# Model Railway Constructor SPECIAL

Ian Allan

## 6. Locomotive kits

### S. W. Stevens-Stratten

First published 1984

ISBN 0 7110 1301 2

All rights reserved. No part of this book may be reproduced or transmitted in any form or by any means, electronic or mechanical, including photocopying, recording or by any information storage and retrieval system, without permission from the Publisher in writing.

© Ian Allan Ltd 1984

Published by Ian Allan Ltd, Shepperton, Surrey; and printed by Ian Allan Printing Ltd at their works at Coombelands in Runnymede, England.

*Previous Page:* **A Wills 4mm scale body kit for a SR Class T9 fitted on to a compensated chassis to Scalefour standards with a KTM DH15 motor. The model belongs to a member of the South London Group of the Scalefour Society, and depicts a non-superheated loco, the Wills kit being modified accordingly. The extended smokebox has been removed and the smokebox wings have been added from thin nickel-silver sheet, also a Drummond chimney has been substituted.**

# Contents

| | |
|---|---|
| Introduction | 2 |
| Tools for Kit Construction | 3 |
| Adhesives | 6 |
| Fillers | 7 |
| Soldering | 8 |
| Prototypes | 10 |
| Plastic Kits | 14 |
| Cast Kits — Preliminaries | 17 |
| Cast Kits — The Locomotive Body | 19 |
| Cast Kits — Tenders | 22 |
| Etched Kits — The Locomotive Body | 23 |
| Etched Kits — Tenders | 25 |
| The Chassis | 26 |
| Painting | 32 |
| Lining and Lettering | 37 |
| Finishing Touches | 38 |
| Some Completed Kits | 39 |
| Manufacturers | 47 |

# Introduction

The first reason why most modellers wish to construct a white metal or an etched brass kit is because it is offering a prototype for which there is no proprietary made model in ready-to-run form. Such kits are made by the smaller firms and are usually of prototypes for which, for one reason or another, the large proprietary manufacturers have felt there is insufficient demand and that sales would not reach the target necessary to offset their very high costs in production and marketing.

Assembling a white metal kit presents its own special problems and requires the development of some basic skills. The first advice for any beginner must be to go for something simple. You may aspire to a Bulleid Pacific for your layout, or have an essential requirement for a Beyer-Garrett but to build such a model for your first kit, without any previous experience, is probably courting disaster. It is rather like learning to fly — you don't take your first lessons on Concorde!

It is therefore recommended that a white metal bodyline kit, which is designed to fit on to a proprietary chassis, should be your first attempt. This will obviate any worries about the fitting of wheels, gears and their meshing etc. You will also have a model which, hopefully, will be a perfect runner at the first test.

Once the first kit has been completed the joy of having successfully built it yourself is soon predominate and it becomes the first in a long line of completed models, hopefully each one better than the last.

It is hoped that this book will not only guide the newcomer into this fascinating hobby, but will give many hints and tips and general ideas to those modellers who are already building kits. It should be emphasised that the text and photographs deal with normal kits and tools and prove that you do not need a comprehensive workshop.

I would acknowledge the assistance given by my colleague, Chris Leigh, who also built several of the kits and supplied some of the illustrations.

S. W. Stevens-Stratten

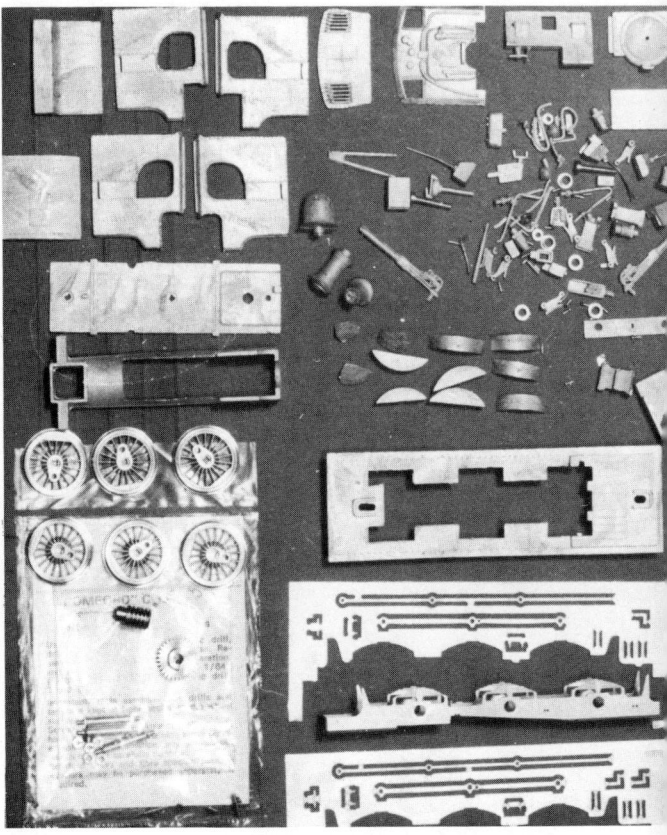

*Above:* **A Westward kit for a GWR 0-6-0PT. The kit can be assembled to depict the Class 54xx or Class 74xx, hence the choice of cabsides and the different splashers. The kit contains an etched chassis, but the wheels and gears are not included.** *S. W. Stevens-Stratten*

# Tools for Kit Construction

You do not need a well equipped workshop to assemble a model kit — a few hand-tools are all that is required. In the smaller scales with which we are concerned there is no heavy work, so there is no need for a lathe, milling machine or large power drill, although a small electric mini-drill working off a 12V controller can be useful as described later. It is not necessary to have all the tools mentioned below and they can be built up gradually after the essential ones are acquired, but one point should be stressed — buy the best you can afford. Good tools will last longer, will achieve better results and will cause less frustration, for there is nothing worse than seeing a good job spoilt by an inadequate tool or instrument.

Similarly a strong and heavy workbench is not necessary and, providing all four legs sit firmly on the floor, the kitchen table is adequate. However, for domestic peace it is a good idea to place a piece of chipboard on the top as a working surface! This can be clamped down with G clamps if necessary and then one can saw and file on this material with impunity — it is cheaper to replace than a Formica working surface!

The tools can be kept in a stout card or plastic box or there are several commercial tool holders and 'caddies' available from DIY shops which are ideal for keeping everything together and yet readily accessible. At the end of a working session it is easier to pick up one item, or a couple of boxes, than have everything loose in one's hand. Empty plastic litre-size ice cream containers are also very useful for storage purposes.

Always keep tools clean and sharp. The soft metal used for castings very quickly clogs the small Swiss files; so after use — and sometimes during use — they should be cleaned with a wire brush to remove the particles of metal that are trapped in the grooves of the file. Small twist drills will also get their flutes clogged with metal and this should be removed before they are used again or they will 'tear' into the metal or plastic sheet rather than make a neat and accurate hole.

Below is a list of some of the tools the kit builder will need, the first part being considered as more or less essential but the remainder are still useful and not necessarily luxuries.

**Vice:** A decent vice is essential and is used for holding parts while being filed or cut, clamping parts while being soldered or glued, as a press in conjunction with a wheel press and in some situations as a tool holder. A vice with jaws of about 2.5in or 3in length, opening about the same distance is ideal, and it is a good idea to purchase a pair of clip-on smooth plastic or fibre jaws at the same time. These are most useful as they will firmly hold small pieces of metal (or plastic) without making any marks on them which the normal steel jaws might cause if the vice is screwed up tight.

If you are using a workbench then the vice can be bolted to the bench as a semi-permanent fixture, but if the kitchen table is used, then a vice which has its own screw clamp is ideal as it can be taken on and off at will. One manufacturer makes a suction type vice which will adhere to any smooth flat surface and as heavy pressure is rarely required in small scale modelling this type is quite satisfactory. Also available are vices which are mounted on a large ball-and-socket so that the head can be swivelled and clamped to any angle. This will allow the user to get round the work at a comfortable position, but generally speaking the normal type of fixed vice is all that is required.

**Swiss files:** It will definitely pay to purchase a decent set of six Swiss files comprising flat, round, half-round, triangular, etc. They can be used on plastic and metal. It is a good idea to keep an old one for soft

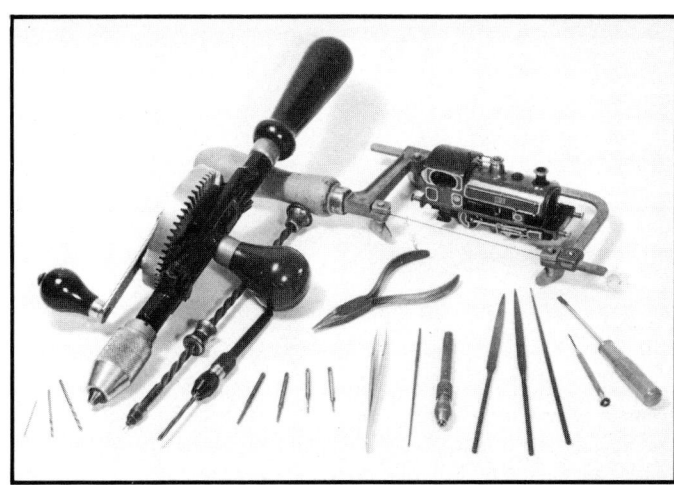

*Below:* **The hand-tools which were used to construct this 4mm scale model of the Peckett 0-4-0ST. The only other item is a soldering iron, which is not shown.** *A. J. East*

metal or removing solder, as this clogs the file quickly. All the files should be kept clean with a wire brush or wire card. If specified, No 0 cut is coarse cut, Nos 1 and 2 cuts are smoother; the higher the number the smoother the cut.

**Small square nose pliers:** Useful for holding and handling various parts, bending wire etc. A pair with 4in blades are ideal.

**Small tweezers:** Used for the same jobs as the small pliers but of invaluable use when adding small parts such as handrail knobs to boilers etc. A metal pair is preferable to plastic because they can still be used on plastic but will not melt if near a soldering iron when constructing a metal kit.

**Sidecutters:** Purchase a good pair that will enable you to cut or snip wire cleanly and accurately. Cheap ones will break or bend the wire before making a rough edged cut. They are also used for cutting the odd snip from a piece of sheet metal.

**Chisel or scraper:** This is necessary for metal kits to remove the odd casting blemishes, pips or bumps, but is also useful for removing excess solder especially on an etched kit. An old chisel with a wooden handle — as long as it still has a good blade — or a professional scraper will do the work, but care must be taken to ensure that the instrument does not slip and cut you. When using a chisel or scraper always ensure that the metal is held firmly in the vice and that you use the tool working away from your body.

**Small twist drills:** Do not use cheap or blunt twist drills for they will never make a clean or accurate hole; likewise never use force when working with the smaller sizes or they will break. Morse numbers 68 and 74 are the most needed ones for handrail knobs and grab-irons etc, but a set from No 50 upwards will be useful. Likewise a set for drilling BA (British Association) sizes from 2BA to 14BA will prove beneficial. Keep drills clean and sharp and they will repay their cost.

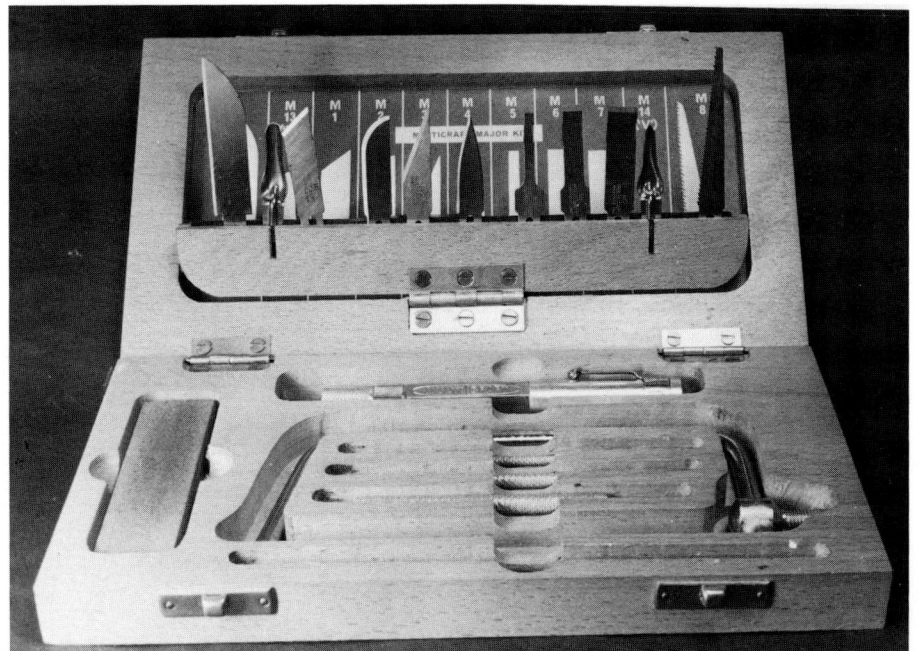

*Left:* **A Multicraft Major tool kit in wooden case. The basis of the kit is the Multicraft Senior Knife which holds securely in a collett all the blades and files. This can then be unscrewed to become the handle for the saw frame, which will also take the Abrafiles. A sharpening stone is also included.**

*Below:* **A hand magnifier on a flexible extension is a most useful item when working on small parts, and is especially useful for lining a completed model. The advantage of this type of accessory is that it will leave both hands free and does not induce eye-strain.**

**Pinchuck:** This is a small chuck mounted on a spindle and capable of holding small twist drills which can then he held in the hand and turned by rotating finger and thumb to produce a small hole particularly in plastic. The pin chuck can be placed in the larger chuck of a hand-drill, but be careful if you do because the user will not have the feel of the tool and too much pressure will break the drill.

**Hand-drill:** Not essential but a useful tool to have around for a variety of jobs, unless one aspires to a power drill. Get a robust one with a free and easy action.

**Mini-drill:** A mini-drill working off a 12V controller is a useful tool for cast kit assembly. It is particularly useful for making the holes for handrail knobs or for drilling any parts of valve gear etc. There are several makes on the market such as the Precision Petite, the Titan or the Pebaro and all have accessory sets containing small grinding wheels, polishing brushes and burrs available as extras. The drills can be regulated for speed by the controller and are therefore very versatile and can take the drudgery out of many jobs, like removing excess metal from the inside of loco splashers. When working with white metal remember that it has a low melting point: so if too much speed is used the metal will heat up and tend to stick to the working tool. Keep a medium to slow speed for best results.

**Metal rules:** For 4mm scale modellers a 6in steel rule will suffice, but a 12in metal rule is preferable, particularly if coach building is contemplated. Get one which is clearly calibrated in millimetres on one side and inches on the other. The rule can also be used as a straight-edge for marking and cutting and also for bending components in etched kits or sheet metal if necessary. If used as a cutting edge, make sure the rule is a steel one, for a brass rule is soft and the knife blade can easily ride up on the edge and cut one's fingers to say nothing of spoiling the rule and the work being cut.

**Razor saw:** Essential for making thin cuts in metal or plastic. Buy one which has replaceable blades because the blades do not last forever. Do not try to cut thick metal with this type of saw.

**Junior hacksaw:** This is for heavier work and should be used for all thick metal. The 6in size is large enough and again replacement blades are available.

**G clamps:** A set of three small G clamps will be most useful for holding pieces together while soldering, or joining with adhesives, especially when it is not convenient to leave them in the vice, or more practical to hold them on the workbench. The clamps are inexpensive and well worth the small cost involved. Some types of hair curlers and clips also have their uses for holding small parts particularly when using plastics.

**Instrument or watchmaker's screwdrivers:** Most essential if there is any screwed construction, such as mounting of bogie or pony truck — they are usually sold in sets of four. Make certain you have the right size blade for the screwhead, otherwise you will damage the screwdriver or the metal around the screw hole.

**Magnifier:** A magnifying glass mounted on a flexible rod attached to a solid base, so that it can be angled at a convenient level and work placed underneath, can be most beneficial — even with those who think they have good eyesight. It will leave both hands free, does not cause eyestrain and will ensure that ultra small and fine parts can be accurately located on the loco body etc. It is also useful for lining and lettering.

Another type of magnifier is the headband type, where the lens is hinged to a band placed around the worker's forehead. This type suits some people, but can cause eyestrain after a period of continual use, and the eyes have to re-focus when the headset is removed.

**Wire or suede brush:** Most necessary to clean clogged files and beneficial when used gently on a completed kit before painting to remove grease and dirt and assist in giving a smooth surface for the primer paint. A glass fibre brush is also useful but they tend to wear away quickly and thus are not so economical.

**Wet and dry or abrasive papers:** A sheet of various grades of glass, emery and/or garnet papers should be kept in the toolbox whether working on plastic or metal kits. The papers are ideal for cleaning or rubbing down cast metal parts while the wet and dry paper can be used universally for cleaning and removing surplus material and obtaining a good polish and finish for painting providing a fine grade paper is used.

**Oddments:** Under this heading comes the useful 'bits and pieces' which are an aid to modellers generally. A length of thin and pliable wire is useful for binding around awkward shaped parts, which will not go under a G clamp, while adhesive is setting. A pair of spring clothes pegs are useful as a short term 'grip', likewise a pair of electrical 'crocodile' clips. An old toothbrush is invaluable for cleaning the castings prior to painting. A small tin or bottle of lighter fuel is a most effective cleaner and it will evaporate from the model quickly. Used in conjunction with the toothbrush it will clean away any excess of flux from a soldered joint.

**Centre punch:** Useful for accurately marking the metal exactly where a hole is to be drilled so that the drill does not 'wander' at the start of the boring. The punch can also be used to emboss scale rivets in metal or plastic by *gently* punching from the reverse side of the material. Some centre punches are spring loaded and have a variable pressure.

*Non-essential tools*

These tools are not essential for kit building, but nevertheless can be useful especially if kit building is contemplated as a serious part of the model railway hobby rather than a one-off exercise now and again.

**Protractor, compasses and set-square:** Not often wanted, but a small metal set-square is sometimes necessary to ensure that the cab of a loco is at 90deg to the footplate, or that the tender body sides are at 90deg to each other.

**Calipers and dividers:** Only necessary if the builder is making modifications to a kit or copying measurements from a scale drawing to a sheet of metal or plastic.

**Lathe:** The whole idea of purchasing a kit is that all parts are already formed and merely need minimum of attention such as cleaning or filing before assembly. The lathe is necessary for people who are going to scratchbuild a model, or who need to manufacture certain parts themselves. An unnecessary expensive for the average modeller, a lathe should not be used without a working knowledge of its operation.

**Micrometer:** A luxury item which is expensive and little used in model railway circles.

**Blowtorch:** More for the model engineer than the small scale railway modeller. Unless the reader is intending to melt metal to make his own castings it is unnecessary, although it can be a useful item around the house or general workshop.

**Taper taps and dies:** Most kits have holes already tapped where required and it is seldom necessary to undertake this task yourself. However, the occasion may arise when a hole has to have a thread put in and therefore a 4BA, 6BA, 8BA or 10BA size (or the metric equivalent) can prove a blessing.

*Below:* **A K's kit for a 4mm scale model of an LMSR Class 5XP 'Jubilee' 4-6-0. The kit is complete with all wheels, gears, motor and has a brass pre-drilled chassis side frames and etched valve gear. Like most kits it does not include paint, adhesive, solder or couplings.**
*S. W. Stevens-Stratten*

# Adhesives

The modeller may be bewildered by the great variety of adhesives, glues and cements which can now be purchased, but many are for specific purposes and materials and are of little use for the model railway enthusiast or kit builder.

The adhesives used for plastic kits are dealt with separately in that chapter and generally have little use other than on plastic.

The cast white metal kit will definitely need adhesives, even if it is partly completed by soldering, while some of the delicate cast parts supplied with etched brass kits will benefit from being secured with an adhesive rather than a soldered joint.

There is one criterion for any kit construction, whatever the material and whichever adhesive is used — and that is cleanliness. Very few adhesives will make a good bond if there is dirt or a film of oil or grease on the surface to be joined. Make certain that the surfaces are spotlessly clean by rubbing lightly with a file, a piece of emery cloth (fine grade) or a suede brush (the type of brush used for cleaning suede shoes which has fine brass wire bristles). Avoid handling the cleaned surface with your fingers, for it is surprising how the grease on one's skin can form a film on the material and act as a barrier for the adhesive. This is particularly noticeable with brass and some of the cyanoacrylate adhesives. Grease can also be removed with a cloth on which a few drops of lighter fuel have been applied.

Another important point is to ensure that the surfaces 'mate' together perfectly. It is unfair to expect any form of glue to make a strong bond when it is bridging a gap and acting as a filler for holes and badly fitting parts. Make certain that all parts are filed for a good close fit. You should always remember the definition of the word adhesive . . . 'A substance capable of bonding materials together by surface attachment' — which means the adhesive must adhere and stick rigidly to the surface. This makes aluminium — with a glass-like polished surface — very difficult to stick to itself and one of the impact types of adhesive is best for this material.

For general use one of the twin-epoxy type resins will prove to be most satisfactory and the quick setting or 'five-minute' type is very effective. This type is 'touch-dry' or handleable in about five minutes (depending on temperature) and reaches maximum strength in about two hours, as against the 24 hours of the regular epoxy resins. There are several brands available from model, hardware or DIY shops — Araldite, Britfix 19, Devcon etc.

The five-minute type (and the regular) can be speeded up still further by holding the parts under the warm air from a hair dryer, when it will be found they can be handled in about three minutes or so. The epoxy resins are in two tubes, one the adhesive and the other the hardener; equal portions of both are squeezed onto a piece of scrap metal or plastic and thoroughly mixed together. Do not mix too much at the one time, or it will set before it is used, and like mustard the makers will be paid more for what is thrown away than what is consumed! When the two parts have been thoroughly mixed the resultant paste is smeared along the surfaces to be joined with the end of a matchstick or some form of spatula. Toothpicks are useful for this as the piece of wood can be thrown away after use. The two parts should now be held or clamped together for five minutes or so — the longer the better — and a strong joint will be made. This adhesive will bond together cast white metal, most other metals, plastic, hardwood, ceramics, glass, pottery and the like, either with each other or with other materials. Another advantage of this type of 'glue' is that it will act as a filler and help to seal joins which are less than perfect — providing the gap is not too wide and that there is good contact at some other part of the joint.

A similar type of ahesive but with one of the two parts being liquid, is Bostik M890. Here each surface is smeared with one of the two parts and then brought together. A strong bond is made in 10 minutes. This adhesive is excellent on metals, but due to the 'greasiness' of white metal it does not make such a strong joint as the other types mentioned above.

One of the modern types of adhesive is the cyanoacrylate group which seem to be known as Superglue or Superbond. These liquids will form a very strong bond within seconds, but care must be taken because they will also stick your fingers together or to the metal you are holding. They must be stored upright in a well stoppered bottle or tube and preferably kept at a low temperature — the bottom of a refrigerator or cold cabinet is ideal. They have the advantage that the bond is made within 10-20 seconds and thus parts need only be held for this length of time without movement. A few spots along the joint is all that is needed as capillary action will make the fluid run along the joint. It must be used sparingly and make certain it does not run onto your fingers. It is useful for tacking together awkward shaped parts, which can then have a smear of twin epoxy resin, or even be soldered.

Impact or contact adhesives also have their uses and some people prefer to use these older forms of glue. Trade names within this group are Evo-Stik, Bostick 1, Uhu and Pafra. Evo-stik is one of the few adhesives which will stick aluminium and is ideal for this material, although it can also be used with cast metal. For the best results coat both surfaces with a thin and even film of the adhesive and then wait until it becomes tacky — almost dry — which may take about 15min depending on temperature and humidity. At this point bring the two parts firmly together and hold for a few seconds and a permanent joint will be effected.

A modern technique is to use a stick of adhesive in a hot melt gun which is a good general purpose tool. However, when used on cast metal there is not quite so much strength as is obtained with other adhesives, although it is very useful for 'tacking' parts together as they can be hand held and the hot glue sets within seconds. A touch at each end of the parts to be joined together will hold them firm and then an epoxy type resin can be used or in the case of an etched kit the parts can be soldered without fear of them moving.

Finally, remember that all parts must be kept clean; they should be held or clamped together; that maximum strength is only achieved after a length of time and until then the parts must be handled carefully. With all adhesives any surplus which has oozed from the joint should be cleaned off, either before it has set, or else filed away once it is hard. Remember, blobs of adhesive left on the surface will show up however well the finished kit is painted.

*Below:* **The two halves of the boiler in the Model Loco Ltd cast metal kit for the LMSR 'Duchess'. These parts can easily be joined by using one of the quick-setting epoxy resins.** *S. W. Stevens-Stratten*

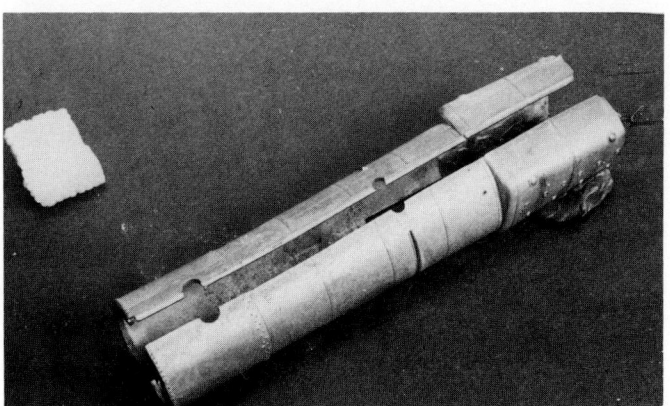

# Fillers

*Above:* **The workbench of a typical gauge O enthusiast with model locomotives under construction, being repaired or awaiting some modification. Note the soldering iron and stand on the right of the illustration.** *D. Featherstone*

During the construction of a cast metal kit, there are, inevitably, a few bad joints where two adjacent parts do not quite butt up against each other to make a perfect join. Such joints will show when the model is painted and therefore they must be filled and filed down so that no joint is showing. Most people have, at some time or another, used plastic wood for various jobs around the house and the same basic procedure is used with fillers for models. Plastic kits rarely need any filling, unless the constructor has been careless or a small part has become broken during assembly, but there are situations which can arise with the construction of an etched metal kit when a little filler can be used with advantage, such as the join between the boiler barrel and the firebox, or the join of the boiler and the smokebox saddle — a sliver of filler will avoid an ugly gap which can sometimes occur.

Epoxy resin adhesive (Araldite etc) can be used as a filler, and if a cast kit is being assembled by this method, it will often seep into a bad joint and automatically fill any small gap. It is easy to file away any excess, but it is essential to make certain that there is plenty of primer across the joint before the finishing coats of paint, as otherwise there can be a change of colour across the join.

There are several types of fillers or putty on the market and the method of application is the same whether it be a two-part compound or a ready-mixed paste. They are best applied with the blade of a craft knife, the blade of a small screwdriver or a spatula. The main thing is to press the compound well down into the crack or crevice and smooth it over. Make certain the surfaces are free of grease, flux or dirt before applying and as several types of fillers tend to shrink slightly on setting it is a good plan to build up the crack slightly higher than the basic surface. When it is quite dry (see the respective maker's instructions on this) it can be filed down flush with a Swiss file, or wet and dry or emery paper. Remember, the deeper the hole being filled the longer it will take to cure and set really hard.

Plastic Padding is very effective: it is a two-tube, equal-parts-to-mix compound in a similar fashion to an epoxy resin. It is easily worked and will file down to a smooth surface with no problems and will be covered by paint without showing. Isopon is another two-part compound, in this case a tin of paste and a tube of hardener, but it is as well to let this really set hard and allow at least 24 hour before painting so that the fumes and chemicals have evaporated. Miliput and Handystrip are also two-part mixtures, but in this case two sticks of a putty like substance are cut off in equal parts and rubbed together to obtain a complete mix. Most of the two-part materials have to be used within five to 10 minutes of mixing.

Ready mixed fillers on the market include Knifing Stopper or Brummers stopping and Cellulose Filler. These are used just like plastic wood, but you must remember to keep the lid of the tin tightly closed, otherwise it will go hard in the tin and be useless. These types of filler are usually sold for car body repairs.

Some of the putties are slightly porous and therefore it is essential to smooth down and prime with paint when dry, otherwise their presence will show when the final coats of paint are applied.

# Soldering

Many beginners fight shy of soft soldering, but, like many other jobs, once you have mastered the knack of it there is nothing to worry about. Soldering can be used to join brass, nickel-silver, tin, copper, phosphor bronze and several alloys with ease, but it is not recommended for aluminium. Silver soldering, brazing or hard soldering comes into another category and is not necessary for small model locomotive building although it is essential for live steam locomotives and model engineering. Soft soldering can be used for cast kits, although it is not obligatory, but it is almost essential if you are constructing an etched brass kit. It is certainly necessary when connecting the electrical pick-up from the locomotive wheels to the motor.

Three items are required for ordinary soft soldering — a soldering iron, a supply of solder and non-acid flux or soldering paste. Years ago soldering irons were fashioned from a piece of copper which was heated over a gas ring, but nowadays everyone uses an electric soldering iron, in which an electric element heats up the copper bit. There is a large variety on the market and all are rated in watts, meaning the amount of heat they will push out — much the same as an electric radiator. The range extends from 15w to 100W and above, but for normal model construction a 25W is ideal for 4mm scale models and maybe a 50W for 7mm scale models.

It is also possible to purchase a 12V electric iron, which has a rating of 15W, which can be operated from a model railway controller. This is most useful as the heat can be varied by the setting of the controller knob and thus it is ideal for assembling cast white metal kits where only minimal heat is required and too much heat will melt the casting.

The other essential is the actual solder that makes the joint which will fix the two components together. At one time tinman's solder was always used in conjunction with a separate flux and while this makes a strong joint it has now given way to Multicore solder which has the flux already embedded in the metal. While the joint is not quite so strong mechanically it is more than adequate for loco kit construction and all electrical work. If some heavier metals are to be joined then the traditional solder and flux will be preferable.

The flux allows the solder to flow easily over the metal surface and prevents an oxide film forming while the actual soldering is taking place. Two of the popular and readily available fluxes are Fluxite (a paste type) and Bakers (either fluid or paste). The latter has the disadvantage that it is corrosive and must be thoroughly washed off immediately after the joint has been made and it is not recommended for electrical connections. For the latter the Multicore solder is unsurpassed for it is non-corrosive. Mention must also be made of Fryolux which is a paste flux which contains solder and thus it is merely painted on the surfaces to be soldered or tinned and heat is applied.

Washing off the flux residue should also be carried out when the model has been completed and before the addition of glued parts or paint, whatever flux has been used, otherwise the chemicals can react on the paint and eventually break, or burn through the finished surface in the course of time. Washing should be done by using a scrubbing brush — an old toothbrush is ideal — with some water and household detergent.

Before a soldering iron is used for the first time the copper bit must be tinned. This is accomplished by allowing the iron to reach its working temperature, cleaning off any dust or dirt for about $\frac{3}{8}$in around the tip and then plunging it into the tin of flux. This will cause a vigorous 'hiss' as the flux melts — if it does not, then the iron is not hot enough. Hold a piece of solder against the tip so that it runs over the fluxed part. When an even coating is on the surface the iron is ready for use. If using only Multicored solder, wait until the iron is really hot and then wipe the solder over the bit followed by a piece of rag (mind your fingers!) so that the hot solder is wiped evenly over the bit.

There is one more most important point for all good and easily soldered joints. The materials to be joined must be scrupulously clean. Dirt, oxidisation, paint and particularly grease or oil must be removed first and the easiest way is to give the surfaces a rub with a piece of emery cloth or a glass fibre brush until they are bright and clean. If there is a film of oil on the surfaces they will benefit with a rub from a cloth impregnated with lighter fuel.

You are now ready to make soldered joints and it is a good idea to practise on some pieces of tinned wire. Make certain both pieces are clean and lay them side-by-side, preferably so they cannot move.

*Below left:* **A Weller soldering gun which provides the correct temperature within seven seconds of pressing the trigger. The fine bit is useful in modelling work, and although the high duty 275W example is shown here, the more usual 120W is preferable for modellers, and even this wattage is not recommended for cast metal. However, it is useful for 7mm scale modellers.**

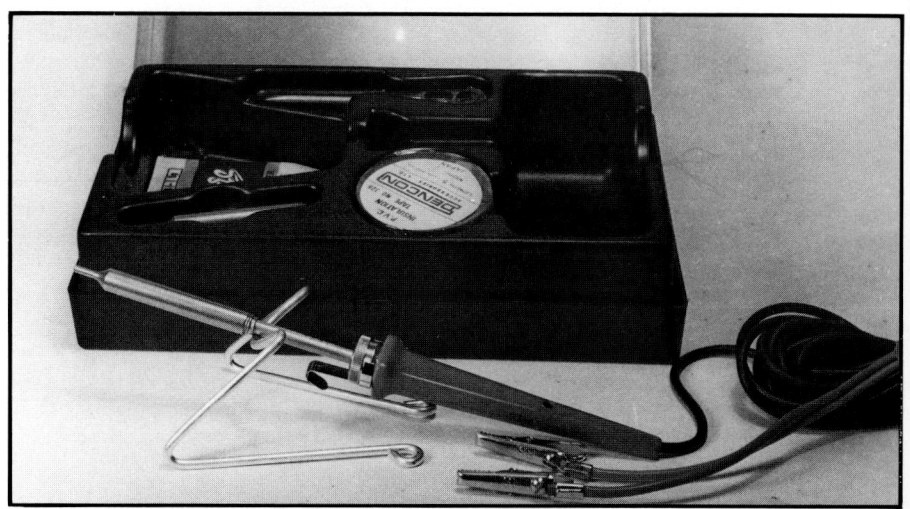

*Below:* **A Solderstat 12W soldering iron which operates on a 12V DC supply — a model railway transformer and controller is ideal. This type of iron is excellent for cast metal kits, as its temperature can be regulated by the controller. The iron can also be clipped to the rails of the model railway layout for 'on-the-spot' track repairs!** S. W. Stevens-Stratten

Make certain the iron is hot — ie a piece of solder will instantly melt when placed on the tip — and hold it on to the two pieces of wire. Within a couple of seconds bring a piece of Multicore solder to the tip of the iron and it will flow on to the two pieces of wire. Immediately take the iron away and without disturbing the wires watch the solder go from a bright colour to a dull silver which will denote the solder has set. This will be a matter of five seconds or so and then the joint is made. Simple! If you are not using Multicored solder add some flux to the two wires before you subject them to the caress of the hot iron and the solder.

Now try with some untinned wire or thin metal sheet. Here it is preferable to tin the surfaces first. In much the same way as you tinned the tip of your iron proceed to heat the surface of one piece of metal or wire and then bring the Multicore solder to the iron and it will flow along the cleaned surface. If you are not using Multicore solder put a little flux on the surface before applying ordinary solder. Allow to cool and repeat the process with the other piece of metal or wire. When both are tinned they can now be held together in a vice or a clamp and the soldering iron put to the two pieces heating them up until the solder or tinned surfaces melt and run together. You may add a little extra flux or even extra solder at this stage if necessary. Remove the iron and allow the pieces of metal to cool. A firm joint will have been made in less time than it has taken to read this. Soldering is as easy as glueing and much quicker, for in many instances, such as making the electrical connection on the metal tag of an electric motor, a mere 'dab' of the iron is all that is required and the job is done.

The construction of a white metal kit by soldering is slightly different. Due to the very low melting point of the cast metal — about 100deg C — ordinary soldering would reduce the cast parts to a mass of molten metal — in other words 'back to the drawing board' in every sense! A low wattage iron must be used with a special low melt solder and a phosphoric acid flux.

Low melt solder is not really suitable for ordinary metals and in any case is more expensive, but it is essential for cast kits. It can be obtained from good model shops and EAMES of Reading and Model Railway Manufacturing (King's Cross) always have a good supply. They can also supply a special liquid flux or you can use a weak solution of phosphoric acid. A low wattage iron (15w) must be used and one of the 12V type running at approx 10V or lower from the model railway controller is a good instrument. It must be kept on the move and should not be kept on the soldered joint a second longer than necessary otherwise there is a good chance you will melt the cast metal part completely. For safety's sake it is better to solder only the thick and chunky parts of the kits, using an epoxy resin or other adhesive for the more delicate parts.

When you become more accomplished with soldering of white metal parts — a practice quickly acquired — you can become a little more adventurous and use the fusing or wipe soldering method. The standard soldering procedure is adopted, but in this case the flux is flooded on to the part to be soldered so that when the iron is applied it actually boils the liquid flux at the same time as the metal melts together and literally makes a fusion weld. Speed is of the essence for once the metal starts to melt the heat must be taken off immediately or the casting will become a pool of metal. When soldering a long seam it is easier to tack both ends thus ensuring that the alignment is correct. Solder an inch at a time working at both ends so that the heat is minimised and not allowed to build up in one place otherwise there could be trouble. This method is not recommended for beginners, but once practice has been gained it is easy, but the iron must be kept moving, and should not be used on thin parts. There is a school of thought that a very hot iron moving quickly does not heat up the casting as much as a lower wattage one that stays in one spot for a longer time — but the best judge of time is experience.

While the phosphoric acid type flux is not really corrosive, it will dry out leaving a hard grey residue which will affect a painted surface. It should therefore be washed off thoroughly with soap and water, making sure that all crevices are reached.

It is perfectly feasible to solder a hard metal such as brass, tin or nickel-silver to a cast part. This is useful because it is sometimes necessary to modify kits. For example, it may be preferable to make smoke deflectors from nickel-silver sheet rather than use the cast ones supplied with a kit which may be a little too thick for realism. This remark does not apply so much to some of the newer cast kits, but some of the earlier ones had overscale thick parts. If you are modifying a kit, you may find that some new parts made from a hard metal have to be soldered to the cast metal and this is no problem. Tin the hard metal in the normal manner, using the ordinary tinman's solder, then place this part against the cast part it is to join. Using the low melt solder, keep your iron against the hard metal part, use a flux and low melt solder and there will be no difficulty in making a strong bond. Do not forget to use the low melt solder near the casting and the low wattage iron and do not hold this too long on the soft casting.

For etched brass kits a normal soldering technique is employed and while it is preferable to add the solder to the iron after it has heated up the parts, this is not always practicable and the solder has to be carried on the iron to the joint. A better joint will ensue if the joint is fluxed first, even when using a Multicore solder, as the flux in this may have evaporated while on the iron.

*Below left:* **There are several stands like this Litesold model on the market and some include a receptacle for a wet sponge, very useful for wiping excess solder from the tip of the iron and keeping it clean. The use of such a stand prevents accidental burns to other material on the workbench, also one's own hands!**

*Below:* **Securing the dome of a model loco by soldering from the inside of the boiler. This cast kit has many assemblies soldered with a 15W Antex mains operated soldering iron.** *S. W. Stevens-Stratten*

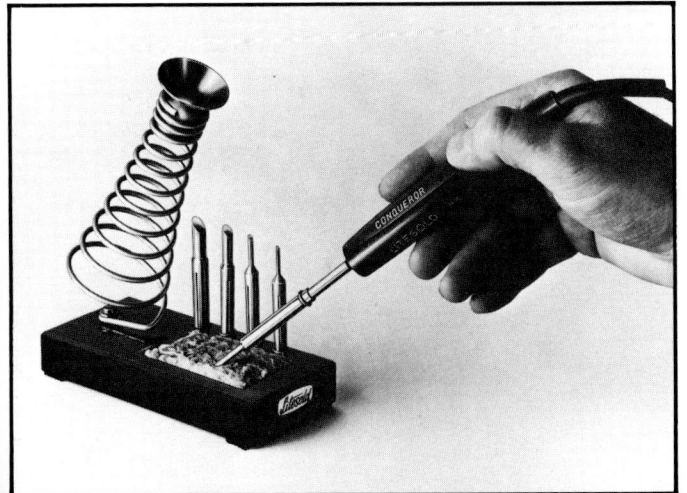

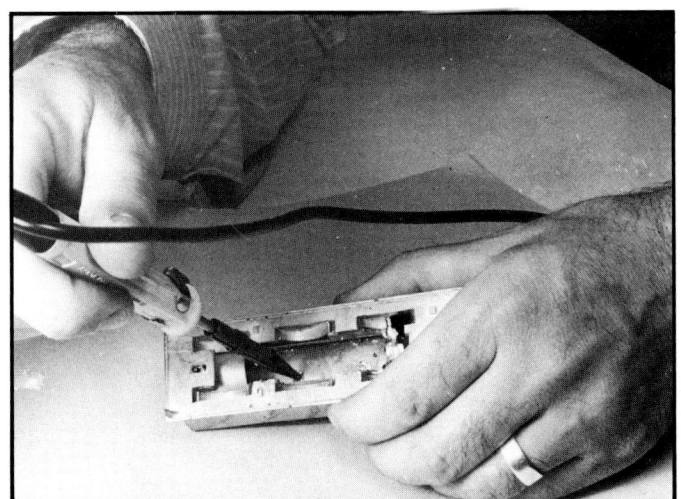

# Prototypes

Good, clear and well defined photographs of the actual locomotive to be modelled are a great aid in completing an accurate replica. If it is not possible to get the actual locomotive make certain your photograph is of a sister engine. If possible obtain a photograph of the locomotive stationary as this has usually been 'posed' with good lighting which will show detail, especially under the footplate.

*Top:* **The famous 'King' class in GWR livery.** *British Rail*

*Above:* **The lining and the position of the lettering is clearly shown in this photograph of a BR Standard Class 4MT 2-6-4T.** *Ian Allan Library*

*Right:* **A view of the cab interior is particularly useful as most kits include a casting of the backhead. This is the cab of an LMSR 'Royal Scot' class.** *British Rail*

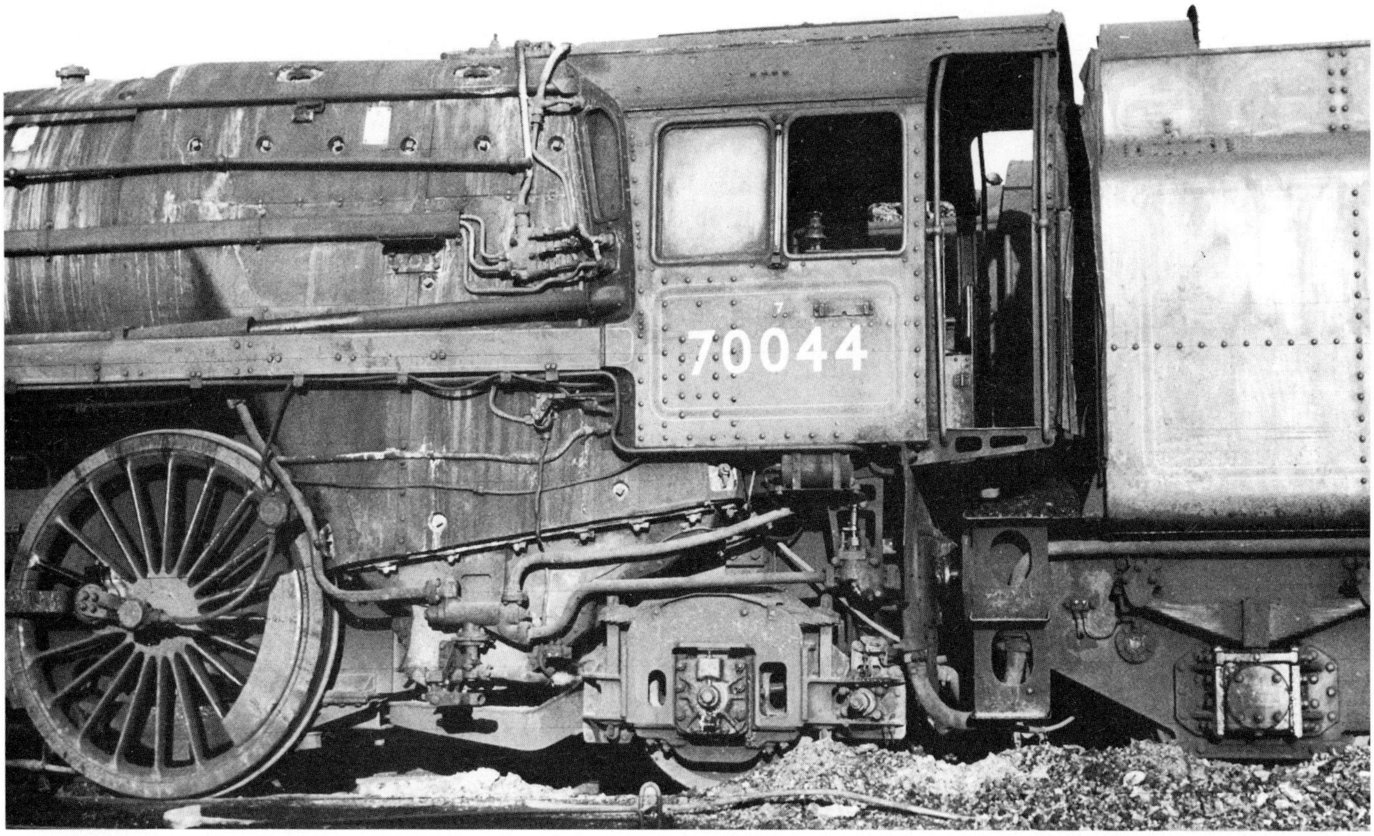

*Above:* **Detail photos are of great value if they can be obtained. This shows the exact position of the various pipes, steps and handrails etc of BR Standard Class 7P6F 'Britannia' class Pacific No 70044 *Earl Haig*. Taken at Bangor mpd in July 1963.** *Ian Allan Library*

*Left:* **The front end of an ex-LMSR Ivatt 2-6-2T No 41290 at Evercreech Jucntion in January 1966.** *D. A. Cape*

*Below:* **The valve gear of BR Standard 4-6-0 of 76xxx class at Feltham (SR) shed in April 1965.** *L. Nicolson*

*Above:* **Photographs of the rear views of tenders are somewhat rare. This is a BR Standard Class 9F 2-10-0 at Stoke-on-Trent in 1967.** *C. Tanous*

*Left:* **The high boiler of the BR Class 4MT 4-6-0 is shown here with other detail as it leaves Southampton Docks and crosses Canute Road in June 1956.** *C. P. Boocock*

*Top right:* **Useful detail, including the livery in LNER Apple Green of LNER Class K4 as built in 1937.** *British Rail*

*Centre right:* **An Adams 'Jubilee' 0-4-2 No 536 in LSWR livery. A useful illustration showing the lining as well as the rivets on the lower part of the tender body.** *Locomotive Publishing Co*

*Right:* **More modern forms of traction cannot be ignored. Detail at buffer height is clearly shown here with many other useful items, such as the 'electrification warning flashes'. 'Warship' class D814 *Dragon* in November 1961.** *British Rail*

LOCH LONG
3441
L N E R

L & S W R
536

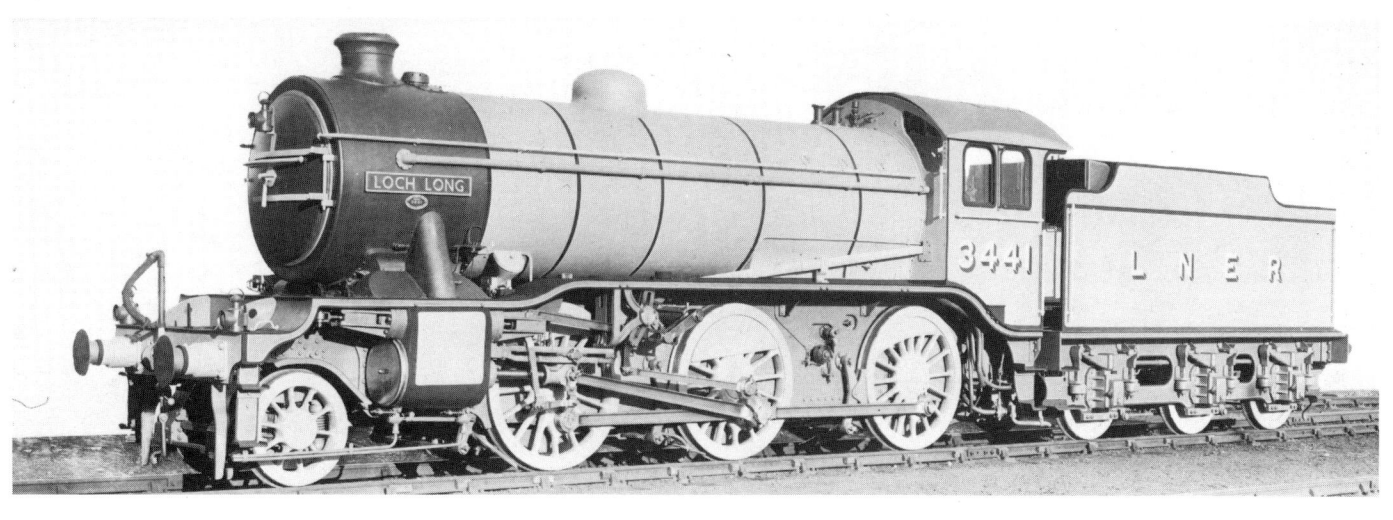

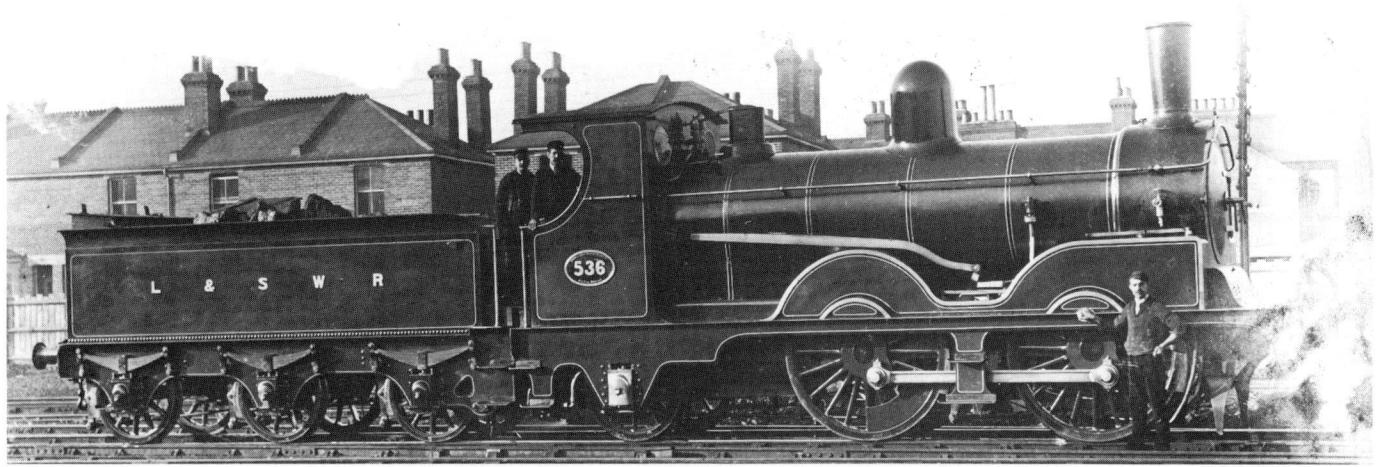

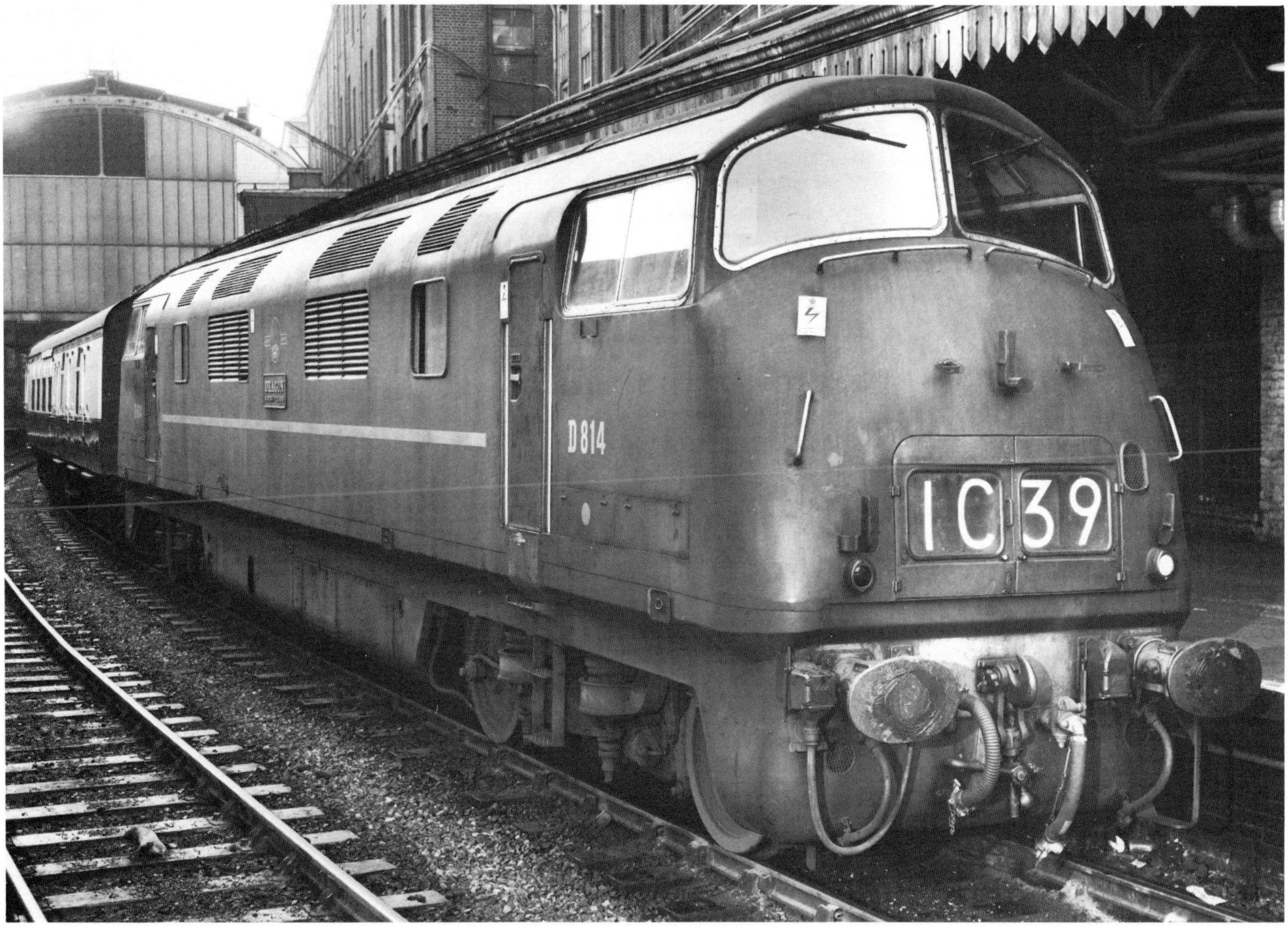
D814
1C39

# Plastic Kits

The injection moulded plastic (polystyrene) construction kit for modellers really came into popularity in the mid-1950s with the Airfix kits for model aircraft and motor cars. With sales outlets in Woolworths and other large multiple chain stores, as well as the model shops, the demand almost outstripped the production. They were deservedly popular for not only were they to exact scale and highly accurate, but the plastic mouldings carried a wealth of detail which was not possible to incorporate with other forms of manufacture or material. All the parts fitted together perfectly; there was no pre-construction work to be carried out — and a tube of cement, a modelling knife, a Swiss file or piece of glass paper were the only tools or materials required to complete the kit. Additionally, as the main part of the kits were moulded in the correct colours, intricate painting of large areas of the finished model was, in many cases, unnecessary. Such kits were a recipe for success as assembly could be carried out by the young novice or the experienced modeller.

The first 4mm scale plastic railway kits were some buildings manufactured by Airfix in 1958 and a year later the first locomotive kit, quickly followed by some coach kits, was produced by Rosebud Kitmaster Ltd. Although the kits were complete they were designed as static models and while the plastic wheels could be made to revolve they would not pick-up any current. It was not long before some of the smaller firms were producing special chassis kits complete with motor and wheels to fit the bodies of the plastic kits. Unfortunately, Rosebud Kitmaster ran into financial troubles and were taken over by Airfix who later produced some of the range under their own name, but alas not the coaches. However, the standard had been set and some other plastic model locomotive kits are on the market including at least four of West German prototypes which are for HO (3.5mm) scale.

There are also some O gauge (7mm scale) plastic model locomotive kits on the market, mostly of American or European prototypes and, of course although larger, the basis of construction is the same.

The first step in the construction of any plastic kit is to open the box and read the instruction sheet and study the exploded diagram. The constructional notes can vary enormously from a fully detailed blow-by-blow account to the now more usual tri-lingual statements and many exploded or sectional drawings. This latter is sometimes a little too sparse even for the experienced kit-builder and therefore the next step is important for all constructors. Look at the pieces carefully and identify them as to what they represent and at the same time see where and how they fit together. Remember that a plastic kit may have anything from 50 to 250 parts and some of these will be quite small and obscure. Having done this fully, you are now ready for the next step. Whatever this stage represents, it may be the boiler, the chassis, or the cab, study the instructions and diagram again and then cut the parts from the sprue with a craft knife. Do not try and bend or twist the parts off the sprue as this will possibly distort the part and will leave a large 'pip' adhering to the edge of the part. So, cut the part off carefully with a craft knife and clean off any residue of the 'pip' which may remain. This can be done with a Swiss file, or it can be carefully pared off with the craft knife — but mind your fingers and always work with the blade of the knife away from you. Plastic can be funny stuff as it will suddenly give to pressure so that the knife blade will quickly gain momentum. With small parts that blade can only be $\frac{1}{2}$in from your finger!

Before applying cement have a dry run and hold the parts together. This will ensure you know how they fit and the best places to glue, but also, but very important, that the parts are the right way round. It is all too easy to cement a piece the wrong way round and this is often only discovered at a later stage when another part is added. The instruction sheets and diagrams do not always make it clear which way round it should be cemented and it will look OK until you realise your mistake later when it may be difficult to rectify.

You now have to consider your choice of adhesive: either a tube of polystyrene cement or liquid solvent which is applied with a brush. There are several makes of cement on the market, all sold in tubes, and there is little to choose between them. The danger with all tubes is that the amount of adhesive straight from the nozzle cannot easily be controlled and, more often than not, too much is applied. This can

*Right:* **The plastic parts still attached to the sprues and the box of the Italian produced Esci kit of the Deutsche Bundesbahn Class 50 2-10-0 in 3.5mm scale. The kit is complete with tranfers.** *S. W. Stevens-Stratten*

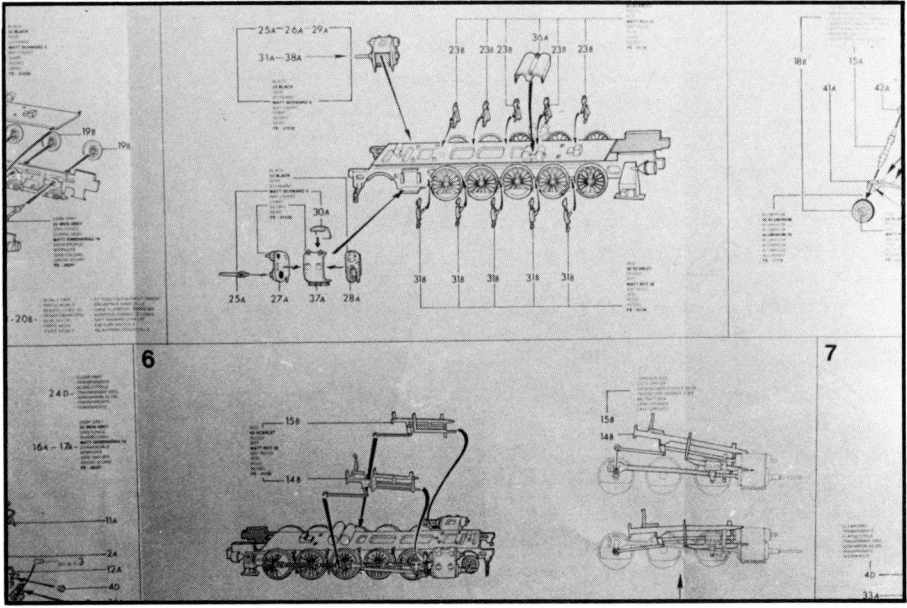

*Right:* **Part of the instruction sheet for the Esci kit. This shows the 'international' type of sheet with many exploded diagrams and very brief multi-lingual instructions.**
*S. W. Stevens-Stratten*

be overcome by gently squeezing the tube (from the bottom) on to the tip of the modelling knife and carrying the cement to the parts to be joined, making sure the residue is wiped off the blade of the knife immediately afterwards. Some of these cements have a tendency to 'string' — that is the cement does not separate easily and the small portion needed does not want to part from the main body of the mixture, and thus leaves a long 'whisker' which will drop on to another part of the kit. This thin length of glutinous cement will leave a dirty mark on the surface which is different to remove. Another danger is that some of the cement will adhere to your fingers so that the next part you touch will leave a perfect finger print etched into the surface — again difficult to remove. However, apart from these dangers which are easily overcome with experience, the cement will form a good hard joint which is tacky within a minute and bone hard within an hour or so, enabling construction to be continued without a break.

The liquid cement is really a solvent which chemically melts the two parts so that they are fused together. Again there are several makes on the market usually called MEK (short for Methyl-ethyl-ketone or a derivative of same). The solvent has the consistency of water and therefore it will run into the joint by capillary action. The bond is virtually instantaneous and finally hard within half-an-hour. The danger here is that the inexperienced will apply too much solvent with the result that it will run 'through' the joint and badly mark (almost etch) the surface on the other side. It is best applied with a brush, and one with long bristles is best so that the tip of the brush can reach right into the joint. Apply the minimum of solution and again make certain that there is none on your fingers otherwise there will be etched finger prints on the surface of your completed model. The solution will evaporate if the bottle is not kept tightly stoppered. If a large bottle is purchased it is better to decant this into smaller bottles so that there is less likelihood of evaporation and furthermore should the bottle get accidently knocked over, there is less to wipe up! Do not spill the solvent on to a polished surface and do not inhale any fumes. It is also advisable not to smoke over the open bottle.

Most of the parts can be hand held while the adhesive is applied, but if necessary some small part may need to be held in a pair of tweezers or even put into a ball of Plasticene which will hold it until the adhesive dries. A small G clamp, or even a clothes peg, is sometimes needed and an elastic band or piece of twine can be useful to wind round shaped parts.

If windows are fitted as for spectacle plates or cab windows, be careful that the adhesive, either cement or the liquid type, does not work through the crack of the join and mark the glazing material. Polystyrene cement applied sparingly with the knife blade is by far the easiest way of securing windows.

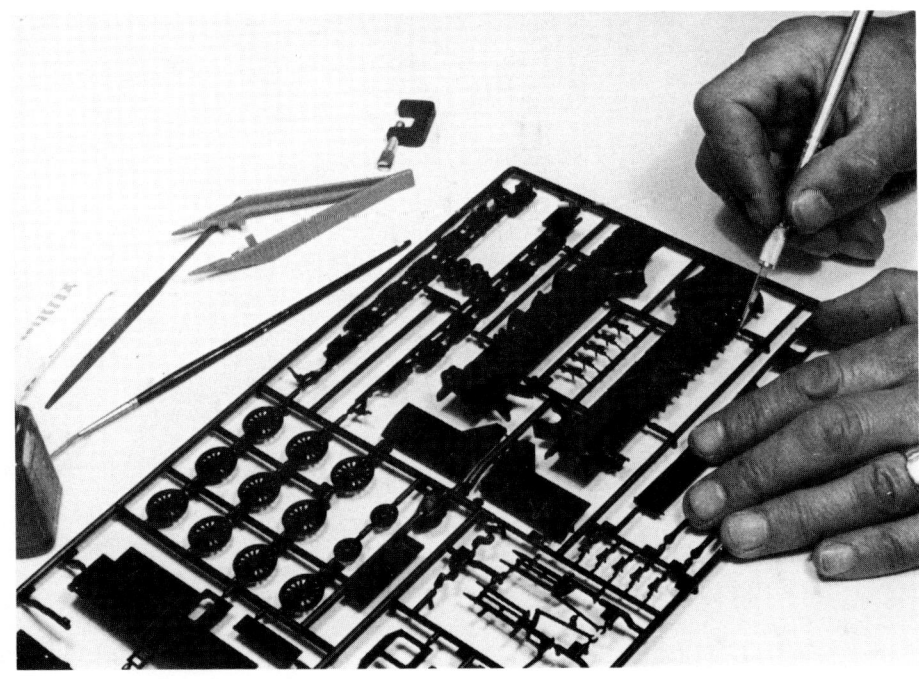

*Left:* **Cutting one of the parts off the main sprue of the Esci kit. Note the part is being cut with a craft knife. Never try and break or twist the part off the sprue.** *S. W. Stevens-Stratten*

Normally there is little or no cleaning up to be done with a plastic kit but if the surface has been marked by excessive adhesive, then the affected place should be gently rubbed over with a very fine wet and dry paper to remove the worst of the mark.

Most kits have their parts in coloured plastic so that there is little painting to be undertaken, but where this is necessary it is often advisable to paint them before assembly, so that parts difficult to reach when the model is completed are already painted. This gives a much neater finish. On a loco kit, for instance, the wheels are much easier to paint while still attached to the sprue rather than when fitted to the model where they are obscured by coupling rods and splashers. They, and other parts, are easier to handle on the flat when one can get all round them. Do not use cellulose paint on plastic unless you have used a barrier paint, because this may attack the surface and give a 'crazed' or 'cracked enamel' type of finish. Matt or semi-matt paints should always be used.

The plastic locomotive kit was designed as a static model and is ideal as a scenic item, that is a non-working model which can sit on a siding or in the loco shed alongside its working brethren. Sooner or later the owner's thoughts may turn to motorising the model either by fitting a proprietary chassis to it or making a special one. Whichever of the two possibilities is followed it is easier if the decision had been made before the body has been assembled. It is not so easy to convert the model after assembly and it may well be better to purchase another kit and start again. Remember you will need a complete chassis with metal wheels for pick-up as well as gears and a motor. There is little of the plastic chassis which could be used, although the main frames are ideal to be used as a pattern for cutting out another pair from sheet brass or nickel-silver. It is not advisable to use the plastic coupling rods, connecting rods and valve gear, as generally speaking they will not stand up to the continual movement. One or two manufacturers were providing ready-to-run chassis for the bodies of plastic kits when these were more readily available in the shops (before the demise of Airfix) and it may prove beneficial to make enquiries from several good model shops in case some are still in stock or can be obtained.

The tender is easier to convert by fitting a motor and in many cases merely requires the new chassis, complete with motor and wheels, to be fitted into the body. A little weight in the tender can be an advantage if tender drive is contemplated, but it still does not get over the problem of the plastic valve gear on the locomotive.

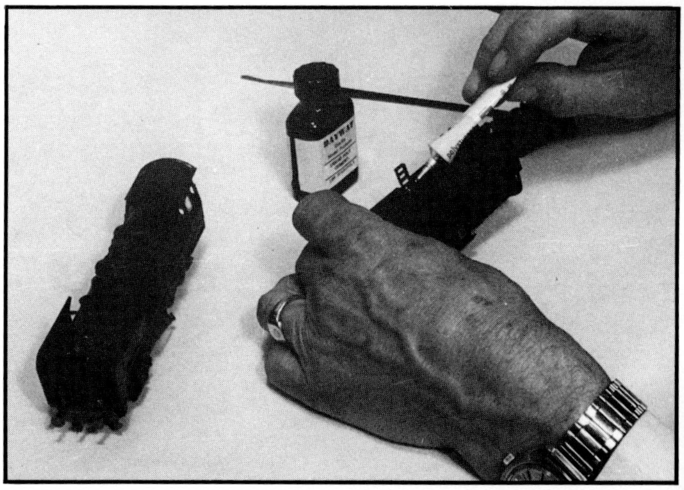

*Top:* **Applying polystyrene cement to the anchoring point for the tender steps. This is reinforcing the 'Mekpak' type liquid solvent in the hopes it will give added strength to a weak and vulnerable part.** *S. W. Stevens-Stratten*

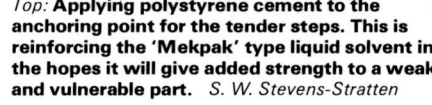

*Above:* **Applying a touch of polystyrene cement carried on the tip of the craft knife blade.** *S. W. Stevens-Stratten*

*Above left and left:* **The completed plastic Esci kit of the Deutsche Bundersbahn Class 50 2-10-0. As the kit is moulded in black polystyrene the only parts to be painted are the wheels, chassis, tender sideframes and buffer beam.** *S. W. Stevens-Stratten*

# Cast Kits - Preliminaries

It should be borne in mind that the cast white metal kit was first produced as an aid to modellers and when introduced in the late 1950s was the only alternative to complete scratch-building, or purchasing a ready-to-run model. It gave a kit of pre-shaped parts, but it was never intended to be the same as the plastic kits introduced later which were moulded to a very high standard in a material which could produce exquisite detail and keep to consistent tolerances of a few thousands of an inch. It was realised by the manufacturers of the cast kits that some work would have to be done on the parts, cleaning, filing and sometimes filling and that they were not producing a kit which was the 'shake-the-box-and-it-will-fall-together' type! Therefore remember that there is some work to be done on the parts.

Before proceeding with the construction of the kit, decide on the actual prototype you are going to model — the actual number, and name if applicable, of the full size locomotive of which you are making a replica. Sometimes there were slight variations in the locos of a certain class and these can be incorporated into your model as it is being constructed. It may be too late afterwards! Details of the actual livery will be needed, not just the colour of the body, but was there any lining? If so, where was it and what was its colour? What was the exact position of the number and/or nameplate and what was the style of lettering and what was the background colour of the nameplate? It is essential to get some good photographs of the prototype you wish to portray so that these points can be seen and checked and your completed model will be as near authentic as possible. Black and white photographs can be seen in books and photographs can be obtained from a variety of sources — it is well worth considering the lists of Real Photographs (Terminal House, Shepperton, Middlesex TW17 8AS). Sometimes a scale drawing will not come amiss and it is a good idea to obtain one if there is one available.

When one starts on construction, remember that cleanliness is important. It is senseless trying to assemble a cast kit on a workbench that is smothered in dust, dirt and old filings etc. The dirt will find its way on to the parts and then it will be difficult to obtain a good joint and, at the worst, it will mean you have to spend more time in cleaning them up. To be methodical is also important and you will work far more efficiently and quickly if the parts are laid out on a clean surface rather than dropped around in among other bits and pieces, tools, tins of paint and what-have-you. Much time can be wasted sifting through a box or pile of rubbish looking for, say, a vacuum brake pipe. Keep all parts in the box and lid which contained the kit, or in other boxes or even on a tray providing it has a deep side.

For the first attempt at kit building it is advisable to start with a simple locomotive design — a shunting tank is a good example — rather than a main line Pacific type loco which has a lot of parts and possibly a tricky valve gear to assemble. Once the simpler — and incidentally cheaper kit — has been completed you will find the larger and more complex kit is much less of a daunting task. If you can find a body kit which fits on to a readily available proprietary chassis, this is best for a beginner and once the assembly of a body has been mastered and you can see the results of your efforts actually running, it will be an incentive to continue with other kits and the construction of a chassis will not seem so difficult.

When you have purchased the cast white metal kit of your choice the first step is to check all the parts against the list of components which is usually included with the instruction sheet. Make certain the parts are all present and correct and identify each piece. Read the instruction sheet through carefully and study the exploded drawing (usually included with most manufacturers' kits) making certain you know where each part goes and then read the instruction sheet again while keeping the exploded drawing in front of you. Some parts have to be fitted before others so you should keep to the order of assembly that the maker has suggested. It is all too easy to assemble a piece the wrong way round (or upside down) and while the part may fit well it will not be apparent until the next stage is reached and a connecting part will not fit. When you are conversant with the parts and the order or sequence of assembly have a 'dummy run' by holding several of the parts together to ensure you thoroughly know how the parts fit and see where it is best to place the adhesive or solder.

At this stage you will find that some of the parts may need a little filing to obtain a perfect fit, you will most certainly have to remove small sprues or casting pips which have been left on. This should be done with a Swiss file being careful not to remove any of the metal on the actual edge, unless of course this is absolutely necessary for a perfect mating of the two pieces. Some parts may fit into slots or grooves and it is possible that these may have to be opened out slightly, again the judicious use of a small Swiss file is needed, until

*Below left and below:* **Two views of a new Westward cast metal kit under construction. The kit can be constructed to depict either the Class 54xx or the Class 74xx GWR 0-6-0PT.** *S. W. Stevens-Stratten*

the part fits the slot. A little paring away at a time is the maxim, do not use a coarse file, and keep offering the parts together until a perfect fit is obtained. Also ensure that parts fit square — for example, the tank sides of a tank loco must be at 90deg to the footplate and not leaning to one side or the other. Again a dry-run is recommended at every step before adhesive or solder is contemplated.

Even though most kits are well packed, it sometimes happens that a piece, particularly the footplate, may be slightly bent during transit. If this is the case the part should be placed on a smooth and dead flat surface — a mirror or piece of plate glass is ideal — and gently pushed flat and then checked against a straight edge.

It is as well to give a thought to painting while construction is in progress. It is sometimes easier to paint parts, which will later be almost inaccessible during the assembly, rather than trying to get a brush round corners or between the bottom of the boiler and the footplate.

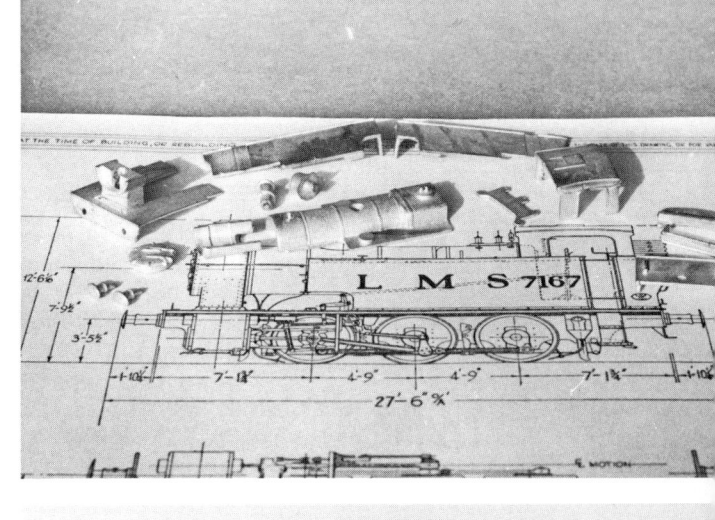

*Top right:* **One of the first N gauge body kits was produced by Peco in 1966. It was for a LMSR Fowler 0-6-0 dock tank to fit on to an Arnold chassis. Incidentally the kit cost 12s 3d (61p) in those days!**

*Centre left and right:* **A completed model of a Caledonian 4-6-0 No 55 from a DJH 4mm scale cast metal kit. The model has been painted and fully lined and is a good example of the need to obtain a photograph of the prototype which shows where the lining was placed and the position of lettering, crest, number plate and etc. This prototype photograph is from the Locomotive Publishing Co collection now marketed by Ian Allan Ltd.**

*Above and right:* **A completed Wills kit of the GWR de Glehn compound 4-4-2, where again the sight of an illustration of the prototype in the period to be depicted is almost essential.** *Photos Wills & Ian Allan Library*

# Cast Kits — The Locomotive Body

Having read the preceding chapters and the instruction sheet yet again, you are now ready to commence the assembly of the kit. The instructions will probably be in two distinct parts — the body and the chassis; but obviously if it is a body line kit for fitting to a proprietary chassis, or where a separate chassis is supplied as a separate entity, then it will obviously only deal with the body.

The body is the easier of the two parts to assemble but there is one criterion which must be kept uppermost in your mind — 'squareness'. All parts must be assembled so that they are absolutely square and/or in line with each other. For example the firebox and the boiler must be perfectly in line both vertically and horizontally, for no prototype loco has been built with the boiler at a slight angle to the firebox (excepting for mountain railways), nor has it ever been pitched to the left or the right! Ensuring that parts are square is not difficult, but remember to look at it from all angles. It may look in line from above, but when you look at it from eye level you may find it tilted up or down. Whether soldering or using an adhesive you may find it easier to make an improvised cradle by placing blocks of wood or something similar under the boiler while working on the parts, and certainly while the adhesive is setting.

It is not possible to give a recognised order for the assembly as practically every kit is different depending on the prototype it depicts. For instance, most tank locomotive kits commence with the fixing of the tank sides and cab front to the footplate, while a tender loco kit may start with the firebox and boiler. The order of assembly should be worked through in strict accordance with the instructions as there is usually a good reason for the manufacturer to specify the sequence they have suggested so that parts can be fitted easily and one part does not impede access to another part which has to be fitted at a later stage.

*Below left:* **The completed body for a Wills kit of the SR Class M7 0-4-4T. The cast metal kit has received one coat of primer.**

*Below:* **The bodywork for a Vulcan Model Engineering 4mm scale kit of the Drewry shunter (BR Class 04) under construction. The left hand engine cover has the handrail knobs inserted, while on the right hand side cover they have yet to be fitted — only the holes being visible.** *C. J. Leigh*

*Bottom left:* **The completed body except for the fitting of the cab roof which has been left until after final painting so that the glazing can be fitted, and the cab details painted. The safety guard or 'cow-catchers' are etched brass and were soldered to the brass chassis but glued to the cast buffer beam..**

*Bottom:* **The underside view of the body of the Vulcan kit for the Drewry shunter. Note the handrail knobs, which in actual fact are split pins, which have their tails protruding in the space required for the mechanism. The pins will now be trimmed off having first being secured with adhesive.**

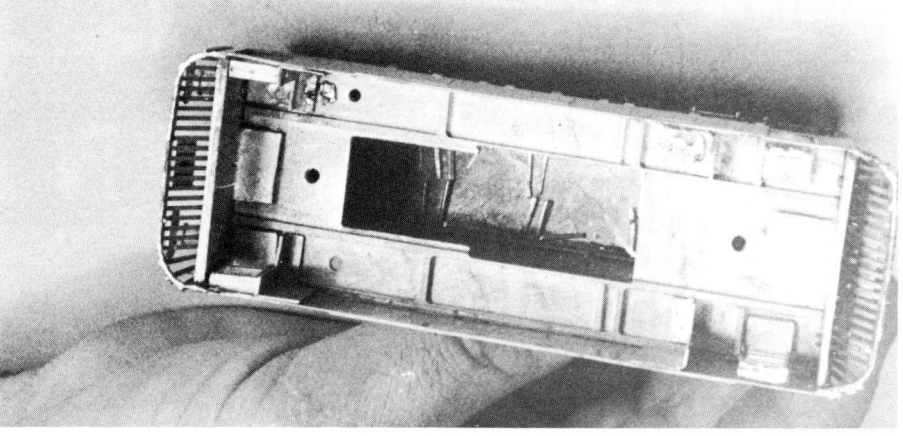

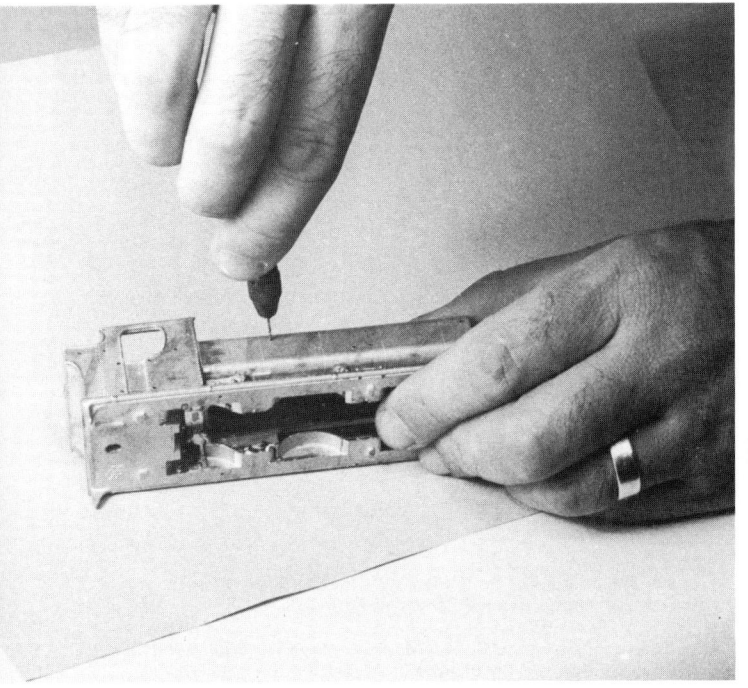

*Left:* **Drilling the holes for the handrail knobs. A No 68 drill in a pin-chuck is being used. The kit is the Westward 4mm GWR Class 54xx/74xx 0-6-0PT.** *S. W. Stevens-Stratten*

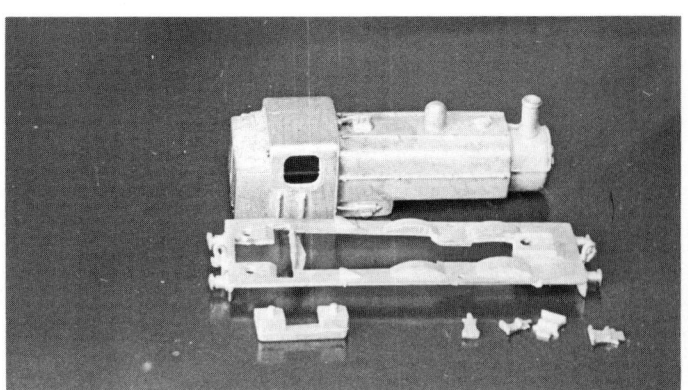

*Below:* **The D&M Castings kit for an N gauge LNER Class J52 0-6-0T body is unusual as the whole body is cast as one piece. The complete body kit is therefore limited to only a few parts — the body, footplate (which is complete with buffers and vacuum pipes), steps and small block for adhesion. The body is designed to fit the Graham Farish pannier tank chassis.**

Assuming the chapter on preliminary work has been read and the instruction sheet and exploded diagrams clearly understood, there should be no problems with the assembly so therefore we will deal with some of the areas of difficulty which *could* arise and give a few hints and tips.

The footplate must be absolutely flat, but sometimes this may be bent or even slightly twisted as a result of transit damage. If this occurs — likewise on tank sides etc — the offending part should be placed on a dead flat surface and gently pressed with the fingers until it is perfectly level. It is a good idea to work on a sheet of $\frac{1}{4}$in plate glass to ensure that all surfaces are always flat and this, of course, is also an aid in getting parts square on. However, do not put a soldering iron down on to the glass!

The cab floor and cab sides should present no problems, but it may be preferable not to glue the cab roof on at this stage so that the cab interior and the backhead detail can be painted at a later stage, to say nothing of adding the glazing. This is particularly applicable for a tank loco where the rear of the cab and the bunker completely prevent any access.

The fitting of the chimney, dome, safety valves and possibly the whistle should not be rushed. Make certain they are a perfect fit and that the flair of these parts accurately fits the contour of the boiler. If not use a piece of emery paper and gently round to shape to remedy any misfit. Keep checking by placing the part on its location, for too much taken off is just as bad as having it look like a $6\frac{5}{8}$in hat on a head which should take a size nine! The same remark applies equally to the seating of the smokebox and smokebox saddle. If the whistle is exposed it may be better to leave the fitting until the very end for it can get knocked and break off, and this really will cause trouble! A touch of cyanacrolate adhesive on the thin part is the only answer, but there is not much metal for a joint. The other alternative is to drill out the residue and obtain a new whistle.

At this stage, if not before, you should insert the handrail knobs and most certainly before you have fixed the smokebox door; as once this has been secured you may not be able to get inside the boiler to open out split-pins which may have been supplied in lieu of the turned handrail knobs. In any case even if the latter are in the kit, it is better to glue them in from the inside of the boiler rather than have an unsightly blob of adhesive showing on the outside. Personally, we usually fit the smokebox door on last, sometimes even after painting as it is not unknown to find that additional weight in the boiler is required to aid adhesion, or to prevent the loco from being too heavy at the back end. If this is the case it will have the appearance of a 'prancing horse'. It is a simple matter to add weight if the smokebox door is loose.

Many cast kits merely have a small depression to show where the handrail knobs, or split-pins, should be placed and this means you have to drill the hole. This should be done with a No 68 drill in a

*Below:* **A completed Wills 4mm scale cast metal kit for the GWR Class 61xx 2-6-2T. The body kit can be supplied with a specially designed chassis as shown here. Wheels and a motor are not supplied. The whole of the bodywork was constructed using UHU as an adhesive, while the chassis was built using a twin-epoxy resin.**

pinchuck, held in one hand and rotated gently until the drill has made the hole right through the boiler casting. This is not an onerous job for the cast metal is quite soft, but do not push too hard or the drill will break. Do not make the hole oversize, otherwise it will have to be filled. If the handrails extend round the front of the smokebox in one piece, do not fix the knobs in the smokebox at this stage.

Bufferbeams should be securely attached to the footplate for these will take quite a few knocks in service, but before fitting it is as well to know what type of coupling is to be fitted as it may be necesary to enlarge the hole for the three-link screw coupling or to add a fillet of metal behind the beam on which to mount some form of proprietary coupling. This latter remark is more applicable for the tender or rear coupling. Buffers can also be fixed at this stage but for safety's sake we would advise against the addition of the vacuum pipes until much later as these are fragile and are very easily broken off.

Footsteps are best left until later when the chassis has been fitted and the model is nearly ready for service. Very often the footsteps are made by a butt joint under the footplate and it is a good idea to add another piece of metal behind the footstep at this point to provide a better anchorage.

Small details such as Westinghouse pumps, sandboxes and oil fillers can now be added to the loco footplate and the body generally.

If you are building one of the earlier cast kits, you may find that the cab sides, cab roof and smoke deflector plates are rather thick and tend to spoil the appearance of the model. A tip worth remembering is that the edges can be filed down to a slight chamfer, which will make the edge look much thinner and this can be done with good effect. However, take care not to file into the edge or you will spoil the appearance and make it worse than its original appearance!

The actual handrails, any engraved name or number plates (including maker's plates) and the glazing of the cab spectacle plates, should be left until after the model has been painted.

Wire for the handrails is usually supplied with the kit and it is invariably a few loops of thin wire in the box. This will have to be straightened and the easiest way is to put one end in a vice and then pull it straight with a pair of pliers on the other end. Once the wire is straight and free from kinks, it can be cut off to the right length and pushed through the handrail knobs (or split pins) and a little dab of adhesive on the end knobs will prevent it from pulling out. If the wire has to be bent round the smokebox door of your model, then it is best bent round with the fingers aided by roughly bending it round the boiler to get the approximate shape. If it is in one piece the acute bend from the boiler side to the curve can be shaped with a pair of blunt nose pliers. When it is to the correct shape it can be fitted to the loco and the handrail knobs on the smokebox fitted on.

*Above:* **Awaiting painting and the fitting of a Hornby R152 chassis is the completed body for a Highland Railway Class 29 0-6-4T. The cast metal kit is supplied by Nu-Cast (an ex-Sutherland/Cotswold kit) and includes the parts of the trailing bogie as shown here, laid out on a scaled drawing.**

# Cast Kits -Tenders

For the inexperienced, or novice, to kit building it may be an idea to start with the tender, for generally speaking it is simpler than the locomotive body while the chassis merely has wheels running in axleboxes or an inside bearing chassis, with no gearing or transmission to worry about. Obviously this latter remark is invalid if a tender drive mechanism is fitted, but this is rare for the majority of cast kits. However, the basic principles are the same as far as structural construction goes.

Generally speaking the tender body consists of only six or eight main pieces and assembly is quite straightforward if you follow the instructions and/or the exploded diagram. There should be no problems and the main essential is to keep the tender body square. The small details such as tender water filler cap, vents, vacuum brake pipes etc are added when the main structure is completed and almost the last job before painting.

If handrails are required this is merely a question of drilling the holes (No 68 drill) for the handrail knobs or split pins and securing these in place with adhesive on the inside of the body. The handrails are made from the short sections of wire supplied with the kit and straightened as mentioned in the previous chapter. A minute amount of ahesive placed on the split pin head (or turned knob) will secure the wire in position but this must be a *minute* amount — a tiny drop from the end of a pin is all that is required, otherwise it will show on the completed model.

The tender chassis is usually a complete casting with the wheels and axles (often supplied with the kit) running in an internal bearing or with a keeper plate, the whole chassis being fixed by a screw or bolt into the outer framework of the body.

The wheels may, or may not be fixed on their axles, but either way they must be placed in position before the keeper plate is fixed. It is essential that if metal wheels are used the insulated wheels are all on the same side as otherwise there will be a continual short circuit.

If the wheels have to be fixed on the axles they should be pushed on and fixed with a spot of adhesive on one side, and then on to the other side. A mere spot of adhesive should be put on the inside face of the wheel and axle, or alternatively the axle end can be smeared with adhesive as the wheel is being pushed on. The most accurate method of getting the wheels on is to use a wheel press, or a vice with soft jaws may be used. See the chapter on locomotive chassis, but be sure you get the back-to-back measurement right.

Fix the coupling of your choice on the rear of the tender, but think of this before fixing the bufferbeam in case any alteration is needed. For instance the small slot for a three-link coupling may have to be enlarged and it is easier to undertake this while the bufferbeam is on the bench rather than when it is fixed in place.

A tender looks incongruous without coal in the space provided so some crushed lumps of real coal (if obtainable), or part of a packet of imitation coal (as supplied by most good model shops), should be sprinkled on the coal plate. If a diluted mix of Resin-W or any PVA white woodworking glue (a dilution of 50:50 with plain water) is used this can be dropped on the coal to stick it to the surface and it will not show as it dries transparent. If the model is not being painted black, the coal can be added after it has received it final coat which will obviate having to mask the area while spraying.

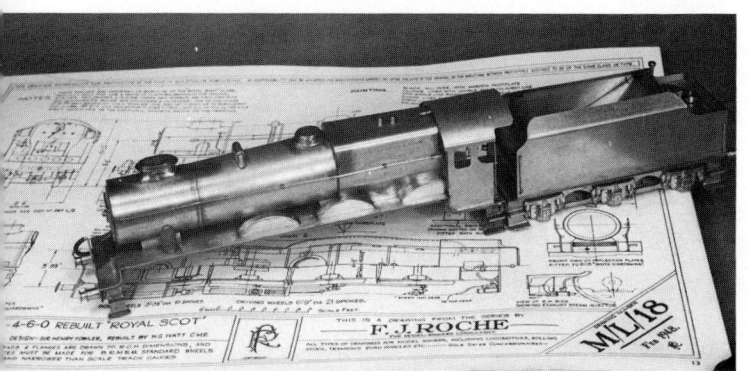

*Above:* **A completed Jamieson 4mm scale brass kit of an LMSR rebuilt 'Royal Scot' 4-6-0 placed on a Roche drawing for the same loco. The older brass kits were very similar to the modern etched kits in general assembly and soldering is virtually essential. The reference to a scale drawing is obvious and this one is included in the book *Historic Locomotive Drawings in 4mm scale* published by Ian Allan Ltd.**

*Right:* **When fitting tender wheels, unless with inside bearings, it is preferable to use pin-pointed axles and cup bearings, which will ensure free and easy running.**

# Etched Kits - The Locomotive Body

The etched brass kit is a totally different concept to the cast white metal one. The process involves chemically etching (sometimes called chemical milling) a sheet of brass or nickel-silver. The process is similar to that used in block making for the printing industry whereby the part required is used like a photographic negative and projected on to a sensitised metal and then acid-etched. Detail can be added by controlling the etching, thus panelled coaches can be produced and items such as door handles are left proud of the remainder of the coach side. When the sheet is removed from the acid it is thoroughly washed and ready for use. For ease of manufacture many parts are incorporated on to one sheet and joined by small pips, in much the same way as the sprue of a plastic injection moulded kit, except of course, the sheets are flat and must be kept so.

The process and use of etching gives strength with minimum weight in the finished model and detail which would be difficult to produce by other methods, a combination which is of great advantage to the railway modeller. In addition parts such as cab sides and smoke deflectors are thin enough to be of scale size, which is more than can be said for cast parts even though these have improved over the years.

In a nutshell an etched brass kit consists of flat sheets of metal, with assembly akin to scratch-building, but having the parts already cut-out and with some detail embossed on them.

Like a cast kit the actual sequence of assembly must be carried out in accordance with the manufacturer's instruction sheet, which should be read thoroughly and studied in conjunction with the diagrams supplied.

The body and the chassis will almost certainly be built as two separate units and joined together at a later stage. The body will probably begin with the footplate and the assembly of the cab. These parts, whichever is the first, must be cut from the fret, but do not cut parts from the sheet until they are actually required for assembly, otherwise they may get lost or damaged.

Cutting the parts from the thinner frets is easily done with a sharp modelling knife with a thin blade, or a modeller's chisel and a mallet; but for the thicker parts, such as those used on the chassis, it will be necessary to use a razor saw. A sheet of hardboard is useful for cutting on. Tinsnips can be used for parts on the outside of the fret, but if used in other places there is a danger of the remaining parts getting bent. Whichever way the parts have been separated, it is essential that any part of the 'pip' which has been left is filed off, as otherwise this may cause a less than perfect joint when other parts are fitted.

One advantage of the etched kit is that parts may be bent or folded over, thus the cab side, cab roof and the other cab side may all be one piece of metal and have to be bent to form the cab body. Most of the kits have an etched fold line on the reverse side, where a 90deg or 45deg bend is required, or a series of etched lines where there is a

*Below:* **A Ravenscale etched kit to make a 7mm scale model of an unrebuilt SR 'West Country' Pacific. This kit has some of the etched work enlarged from the earlier Kemilway 4mm scale kit.**

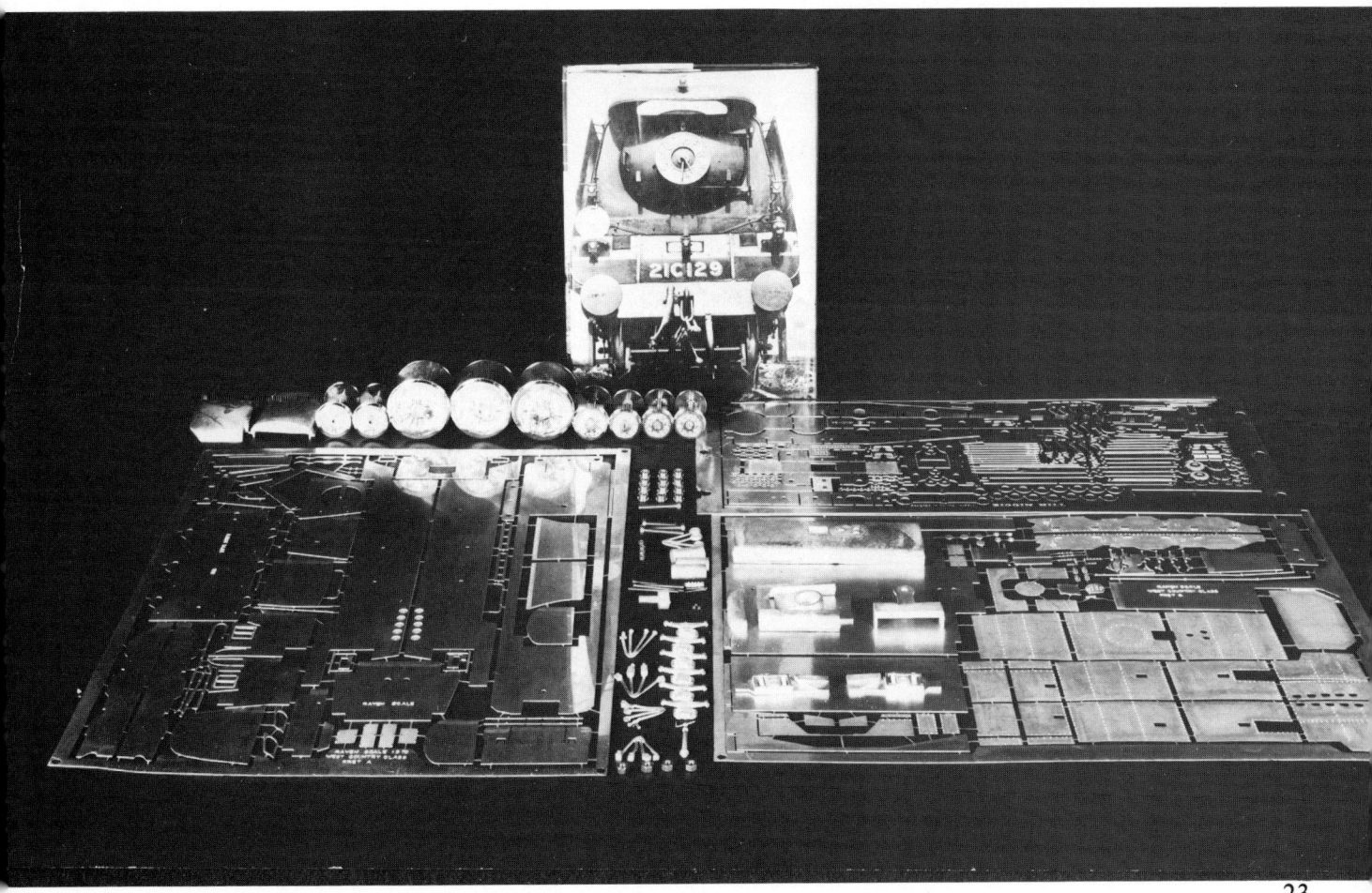

gentle bend. This may appear daunting to the modeller the first time he has to undertake this operation, but if care is taken there is no need to panic.

A straight bend in the thinner brass or nickel-silver as used in say the cab side is easily accomplished. Place the larger section of the material to be bent on a flat surface, the work bench or a table and place a straight edge or block of hardwood along the fold line. With the end to be bent placed over the edge of the bench or table, use your fingers to hold the straight edge firmly on the fold line, then with your thumbs press the metal upwards. The illustration will show this clearly and it is surprisingly easy.

Parts that require a gentle bend or curve can often be worked around a former of approximately the same size. The rounded roof of a loco cab where it meets the side sheets can often be bent round the front part of the cab if this is held in place while bending. It is surprising how often a look around the kitchen will reveal articles that are approximately the right radius to act as a former — round handled knives, small jars or bottles, etc. Make certain that all parts are correctly bent or folded before you solder as afterwards will be too late.

The footplate is often built up in two distinct layers and if this is the case make certain they are correctly placed before sweating them together.

When the cab unit has been built up, it may be prudent to put it on one side and start on the firebox. This is often one piece of thin copper or brass and has to be bent to shape. Formers are supplied and these can be used to get the required contour, but great care must be exercised and the operation taken slowly. 'Dry-run' checks should be made at every stage to ensure that the shape has not got a fold, crease or waver in it, also that it is square and will lie flush with the front of the cab and at the same time will sit squarely and evenly on the footplate.

The boiler shell will usually be a pre-formed piece of brass tubing and the smokebox may be a piece of thin copper which has to be placed tightly round it. If this is the case it should be bent round, obviously using the boiler as a former, until it is a tight fit, again with no creases or folds. It can be sweated on with a high wattage soldering iron, but as so much heat is lost in the large expanse of the boiler it is not such a satisfactory way of fixing. It is therefore easier to fit the 'wrapper' (smokebox) with Araldite or another of the quick setting epoxy resins. A smear of the mixed two-part adhesive is put round the inside of the smokebox and then it is fitted in place and held tightly on to the boiler with elastic bands, or thin wire wrapped round. Make certain that any handrail knob holes and, of course, the hole for the chimney are in line with those on the boiler, then put aside to set.

Assuming the smokebox saddle has been fitted, the boiler can now be placed against the firebox (or cab front) and rested on the saddle. It should be a good and perfect fit all round, square from whatever angle you are looking at it, and with any holes for chimney etc absolutely vertical.

It is important that the smokebox fits snugly in the saddle, if not then file gently until a perfect fit is obtained, checking every couple of strokes of the file.

Before fixing the boiler, now is the time to drill holes for the handrail knobs and any other components which may have to be added — such as Westinghouse pumps, etc. This can be undertaken with a pin chuck and the appropriate size drill (No 68 for handrails). The chuck is held between finger and thumb with a drawing pin in the hollow shaft which will provide a comfortable bearing for the forefinger. It can be a tedious job, but a sharp drill will soon pierce through the metal. A less tedious way is to use one of the small electric mini-drills of which there are many varieties on the market that will run off a 12V model railway controller. Too much pressure will break the thin drill, but it is less time consuming than doing the operation by hand. You can also obtain miniature burrs and accessories like sanding and grinding wheels, which are useful for removing excess solder and generally cleaning up the kit after construction.

*Below:* **Using a chisel shaped knife blade and a very small hammer, the parts of an etched kit are separated from the main sheet or fret. For thick chassis parts it is better to use a razor saw. The fret should be laid on a piece of hardwood or hardboard so that there is no buckling or twisting of the parts being removed.** *S. W. Stevens-Stratten*

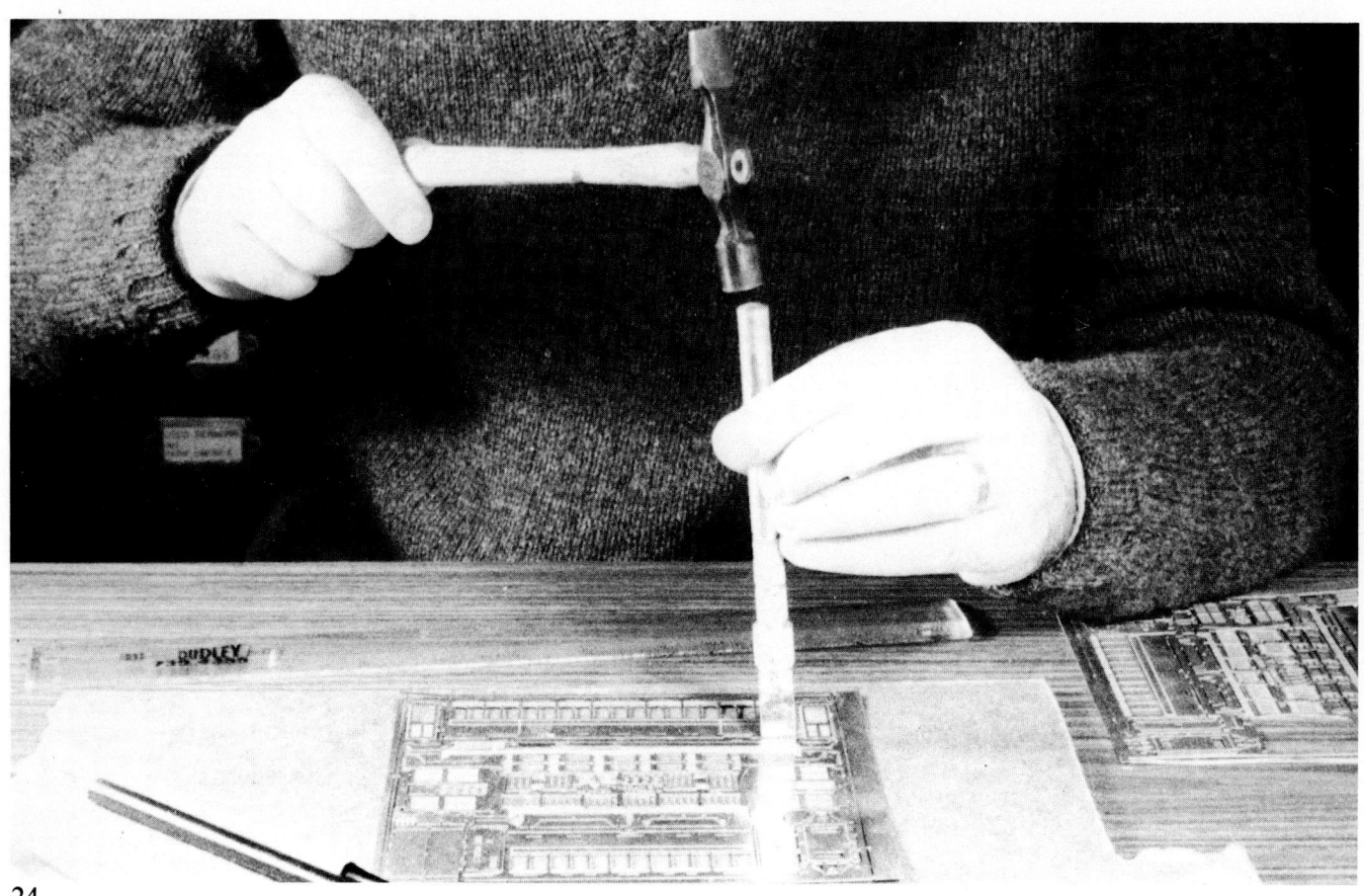

# Etched Kits - Tenders

As with the white metal kits, novices to etched kits may find it a good idea to start with the tender. This will give you the 'feel' of working with etched brass or nickel-silver because, generally speaking, the tender is easier to construct than the loco body because there is no firebox or other awkward shape.

Construction of the tender may vary with different kits, but the usual method is to have the tender sides and back all in one piece of metal which has to be bent and soldered to the tender floor. Score lines are normally etched on the inside of the bend and it is not too difficult to effect the bending whether it be a straight 90deg bend or a more gentle curve. Often a thin pencil (the type that is fitted in some diaries) or a knitting needle of the right diameter can act as a former.

A problem can arise if the tender has a flared top which has to be bent outwards at about 45deg. The difficulty is at the two rear corners where the flare also has to be bent round: in some kits this is catered for by 'notching' or mitring the corner. This has to be fashioned carefully and probably filled in with solder and then filed clean to the final smooth contour.

Etched coal rails are often supplied if it is in accordance with the prototype, but although delicate they are easily added by soldering. Steps are best left to the last as they are likely to get knocked or bent if added at this stage.

Cast metal axleboxes and springs have to be fitted to the outside frame of the tender and while the former can be soldered on, it is not so easy with the castings for the springs if they are not integral with the axlebox. As they are quite small it is easier — and safer — to add them on using one of the twin epoxy resins.

Small details such as tool boxes may be supplied as an etched part which has to be folded up to a box shape from the flat sheet, but this is easily done and a mere touch with a soldering iron is all that is required. Alternatively depending on the kit, they may be supplied as white metal castings in which case they can be added with adhesive.

Tender cab doors which actually work are featured on some etched kits and these should be assembled as per the instructions which is usually a split-pin and wire for the hinge. The doors should just come inside the cab side of the loco. The fallplate is sometimes soldered as a static item, but a few kits have had horizontal movement in these, again using split-pins and wire as an anchorage and hinge.

The tender chassis is usually straightforward, merely requiring two bends in the flat metal and the wheels inserted in the slots provided with a keeper plate soldered over the axles to keep them in place.

However, it is vitally important that the chassis is bent absolutely square and if one side is not at 90deg to the top, trouble will ensue and the tender will have a permanent list to port or starboard. Check this item carefully, also that it is square to the underneath of the tender floor not only vertically but horizontally and that it is in line with the outside edges of the tender body and absolutely central.

The wheels may already be fitted to the axles, or they may be separate. If the latter is the case, push the axle through the centre holes in the wheels using a Hamblings wheel press if one is available, or else a vice fitted with soft jaws. The hole may need to be slightly enlarged, but do not rush at this job like a bull in a china shop, for like so many steps in the construction of a model, it pays to proceed slowly and make a trial fit at every move. The wheels should fit on the axle as a tight push-fit and should not slide on easily. A touch of adhesive will permanently secure the wheel in position on the axle. However, this should only be done when you are certain the wheel is in the right position from the end of the axle and that the back-to-back measurement is correct. Further make certain the wheel is running true on the axle and has not been accidently put on slightly askew. Run the pair of wheels on their axle across a dead flat surface, such as an old mirror or piece of plate glass and watch carefully to ensure there is no wobble.

You must also make certain that the insulated wheels are all on one side, if insulated and non-insulated wheels are supplied. If plastic wheels have been supplied then of course the above remark does not apply.

Brake blocks are sometimes cut from the etched sheet and sometimes are cast, but these should be added as per instructions taking care they do not foul the wheels and that they are straight and all in line. If brake rodding is incorporated this is often made of wire and should be soldered or 'Araldited' in place.

When all the small detail pieces have been added the tender can be put aside for painting. This must be done at the same time as the loco and should not be undertaken as a separate item, in case the paint mix is slightly different. Wait until the loco has been finished and then paint both items at the same time. See the chapter on Painting.

*Below:*
**A completed model of a Gresley designed Class J29 of the LNER. Available in kit form, or as a ready-to-run model it was constructed mainly of brass with lost wax castings. Unfortunately Micro Metalsmiths who produced the models are no longer engaged in the model railway trade.**

# The Chassis

If scratchbuilding was being discussed, we would probably state that the chassis should be constructed first, so that the body could be tailored to fit, but with a kit we can assume that the chassis will fit into the body without undue problems as the manufacturer has taken all this into consideration with his design work. Any interior body projections which would foul the motor would be of a very minor nature and could easily be filed away or covered with insulating material.

As the chassis of the later releases of cast white metal kits are often etched, and even if cast the basic principles are the same, it seems sensible to deal with both etched and cast chassis under one heading.

At the risk of repeating ourselves, it is even more imperative to ensure that everything on the chassis is square. Follow the makers' instructions implicitly with regard to procedure and order of assembly, for there is a wide variation in ideas between different kits.

There are four main types of loco chassis. First there is the block of cast white metal (or an alloy casting) with the necessary slots for motor and gear fixing and the holes for the axles already drilled and bushed. The bushes are usually of brass, or phosphor bronze, and take the wear of the revolving axle, otherwise the round hole would soon turn into an oval in the soft white metal.

Another form of chassis is supplied as $1/16$in brass frames pre-cut and drilled which are screw assembled to cross-members or spacers. The newer K's kits employ this method of chassis construction.

Some kit manufacturers have provided chassis which are milled from solid brass, but again the axle holes, slots for motor and gears are already drilled or shaped.

The last type of chassis now being used extensively for both cast and etched kits is the etched chassis. This has to be detached from the sheet of brass or nickel-silver and is usually in one piece which has to be bent to form the two sides and top. As this is etched in a much thicker material than the body parts, it is almost essential that the bending be undertaken in a vice, for it is necessary to get the side frames exactly at 90deg to the top. This fold-up type of chassis is not so easy if the finished model is to be for EM gauge, for this will necessitate washers being put between the inside of the driving wheel and the actual chassis to take up the extra play which will occur.

Another variation on the etched chassis is for the side pieces to be etched on the flat sheet but instead of being folded over the side pieces are removed and spacers of the requisite distance (for HO/OO or for EM gauge) are soldered or screwed to the side frame. If this technique is adopted for the chassis make certain the spacers are soldered square and that the side frames are also square and both sit properly on a flat surface such as a piece of plate glass.

Whichever type of chassis is supplied with the kit you should remember that it is virtually the heart of the locomotive and great care should be taken in its assembly if perfect running is to be obtained.

It will be much easier to paint the chassis matt black before wheels, axles, motors and gears are fitted. The chassis can be brush painted or sprayed with an aerosol can, as it is barely worth getting an airbrush fitted-up, assuming you have one, for this small job. It's also easier to paint the wheels on the flat, than waiting until they are partly obscured by coupling rods and valve gear.

Wheels are usually fitted at the next stage and here again there are variations in fixing according to the different manufacture.

K's wheels have a 'D' shaped centre hole which fixes over similar shaped ends on their shouldered axles. This makes wheel quartering an easy matter and when the screws holding the wheel to the axle are tightened they remain firmly in place. The wheels also have 14BA screws in the boss so that the connecting and coupling rods are placed over these and a nut keeps them in position.

Hambling's wheels are made for a push fit on to their splined and shouldered axles and crankpins are already fitted. The wheels have metal rims and centres with plastic spokes.

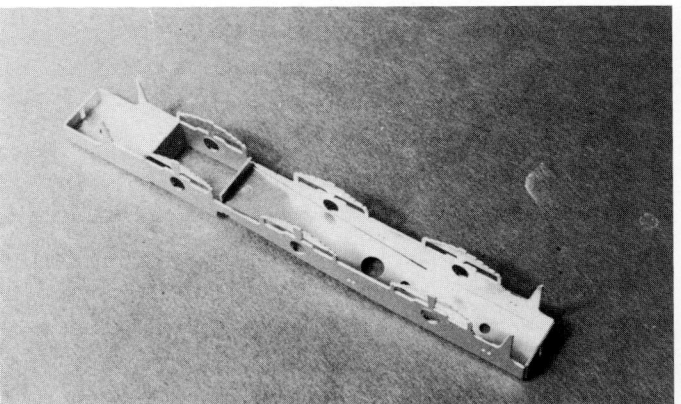
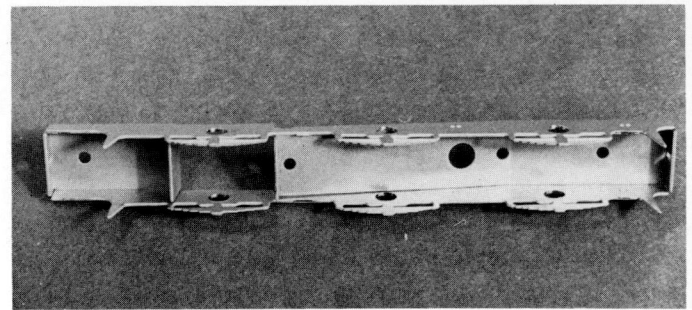

Romford wheels have a square axle fitting and their axles have square cut shouldered ends which again aid quartering, prevent the wheels slipping on the axles and aid the correct back-to-back measurement. The wheels are held by lock nuts and the crankpins are 10BA screws with washers to be soldered on.

Once tight all wheels should be finally secured with a minute touch of adhesive to prevent them from working loose.

Much is talked about the correct quartering of driving wheels, but much less is written about the subject. In actual fact it is not as difficult as some people will lead you to believe. To obtain the correct quartering, which will help the free-running of your model, the right-hand side, looking from the rear or driver's cab, must lead by 90° with the wheels turning for a forward movement. Remember the wheels are turning towards the cab. In actual fact this means that when the coupling rod on the left hand side is at the bottom of its travel, or in other words the crankpins are right down or at a 6 o'clock position looking side on, the right-hand coupling rods should be half way up the wheels and thus the crankpins will be at 9 o'clock, looking side on. There may be a few prototype exceptions to this rule, but it works well for all models. It, of course, applies to all the driving wheels of a locomotive and whether it is a four-coupled or an eight-coupled the wheels must all be in exactly the same place on that side. Remember, crankpins left at 6 o'clock and crankpins right at 9 o'clock and you will not go wrong.

If you are using insulated and non-insulated wheels make certain the insulated side is always the same, normally the righthand side looking from the rear.

Do not forget that the gearwheel has to be fixed to the driving axle as it is threaded through the chassis. It is better to leave the gearwheel as a push fit (or it may be fixed with a grub screw) until the other gearwheel or worm is in place. This will ensure correct meshing of gears and that the gearwheel is in correct relationship with the worm on the motor driving shaft. The gear wheel can then be soldered in position or fixed with Araldite or Super Glue.

Where a push fit is required on a driving wheel (or bogie or pony wheels for that matter) this is best accomplished by using a wheel press. Hamblings make one which has been well tried and proved popular over the years. The press not only ensures the wheels slide on to the axle squarely, but it will automatically quarter them and it can be used with the chassis in position. Alternatively, they can be pushed home in a small vice, but be careful not to exert too much pressure or a bent axle will result. If a vice is used it should be fitted with a pair of soft jaws which can be obtained from tool shops. Made of a semi-soft material such as hard rubber, they simply fit over the existing jaws of the vice so that the surface under tension is not marked. On no account should an axle be driven into a wheel with a hammer. You require gentle pressure not a sudden and powerful force which could force it on crooked.

These points made on driving wheels apply equally to bogie and pony wheels — especially if Peco Insul-axles are used as these are made from a softer material and can easily be bent if forced too hard. It may be necessary to place insulated washers on the axle between the inside of the bogie wheel and the bogie frame to prevent a short circuit, especially with certain makes of wheels which are insulated at the axle mounting.

Some bogie and pony wheel assemblies have the axles held in place with a keeper plate. If you are using epoxy resin to secure this, make certain that no adhesive gets near the axle or into the axle slots: this will impair smooth running.

As the driving wheels will be picking up the electrical current from the rails it is imperative that they make good contact with the track at all times, especially when running over points. The ideal would be to have independent suspension fitted to every wheel or axlebox, but this is impractical for small scales, although it has been undertaken in some scratchbuilt models. However, there is one small tip worth mentioning: if you open the axle holes in the frames a little at the bottom — in other words make an oval hole so that the axle bearings can move up and down a fraction, $\frac{1}{16}$in or less is ideal — the wheels will be free to drop down over points or any slight track irregularities. This cannot be done on the driving axle as it would cause the gear meshing to become partially disengaged, but it makes quite an improvement to running if judiciously done on the other coupled wheels.

When fitting coupling rods the elbows or oiling points must face upwards towards the footplate and the body of the loco. Most driving wheels have the crankpins already inserted and it is merely a case of placing the rods on and tightening a nut. If no crankpin is fitted — something of a rarity these days — you will have to glue in a headless soft pin, but remember it will have to be riveted over when the rods are on. Alternatively you may be able to use a 14BA screw with the head removed and then place a nut on afterwards.

When checking the chassis for free running you may find that it is stiff and something is 'binding' somewhere. The first thing to check is the quartering of the wheels, but another cause could well be that the

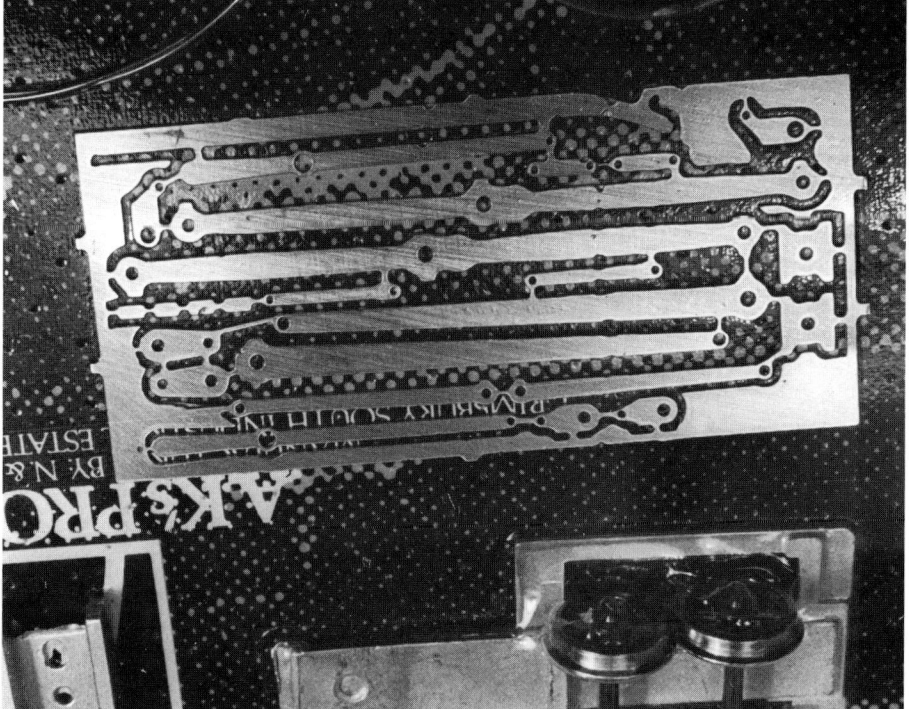

*Far left:* **Bending an etched brass chassis, in this case the Vulcan Model Engineering kit for the Drewry shunter. The top of the chassis is being held on the top of a table by a steel rule, while the side is being bent at right angles over the edge of the table.** *S. W. Stevens-Stratten*

*Above and below left:* **Two views of the etched brass chassis for a Westward kit of a GWR pannier tank. The chassis is assembled completely by folding from the flat sheet which has fold lines etched on to make the task quite easy. It is only necesssary to ensure that everything is at 90deg to each other. The end corners can be soldered for extra strength if required.** *S. W. Stevens-Stratten*

*Right:* **Illustration of a sheet of etched valve gear and coupling rods etc from a K's kit.** *S. W. Stevens-Stratten*

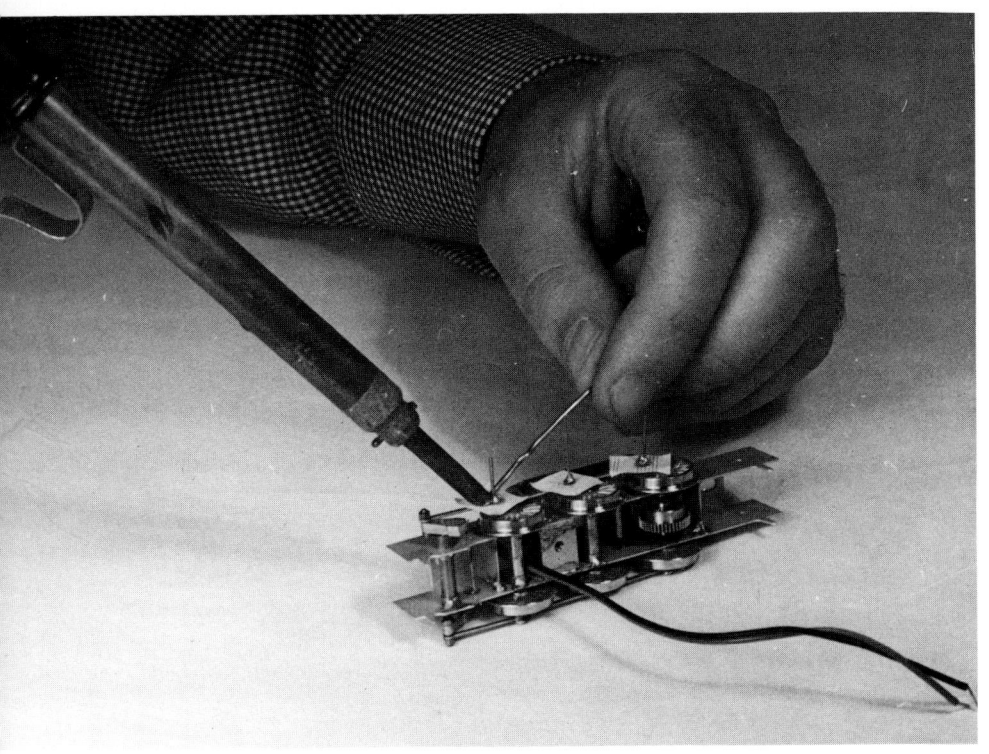

*Left:* **Soldering securing washers on the crank pins of the Vulcan kit of the Drewry shunting locomotive. The paper placed underneath the washer avoids solder getting on to the coupling rod, also when removed it gives a slight amount of play necessary for a free running chassis. The wire to the motor has already been soldered on to the motor terminals and the next job will be to cut it to length and solder to the pick-ups.** *S. W. Stevens-Stratten*

*Below:* **A selection of motors for 4mm scale model locomotives. Left to right on curved rear row are — Anchoridge D13, Airfix 1003, Mashima TA12, Airfix 1002 and KTM DH105. Front row — K's H2M, ECM type 2, ECM type 1 and KTM DH13.** *J. D. Smith*

*Bottom:* **A further selection of motors, left to right — ECM type 3, Rovex X04, MW 005 (the Airfix 1001 is similar), and Romford Bulldog.** *J. D. Smith*

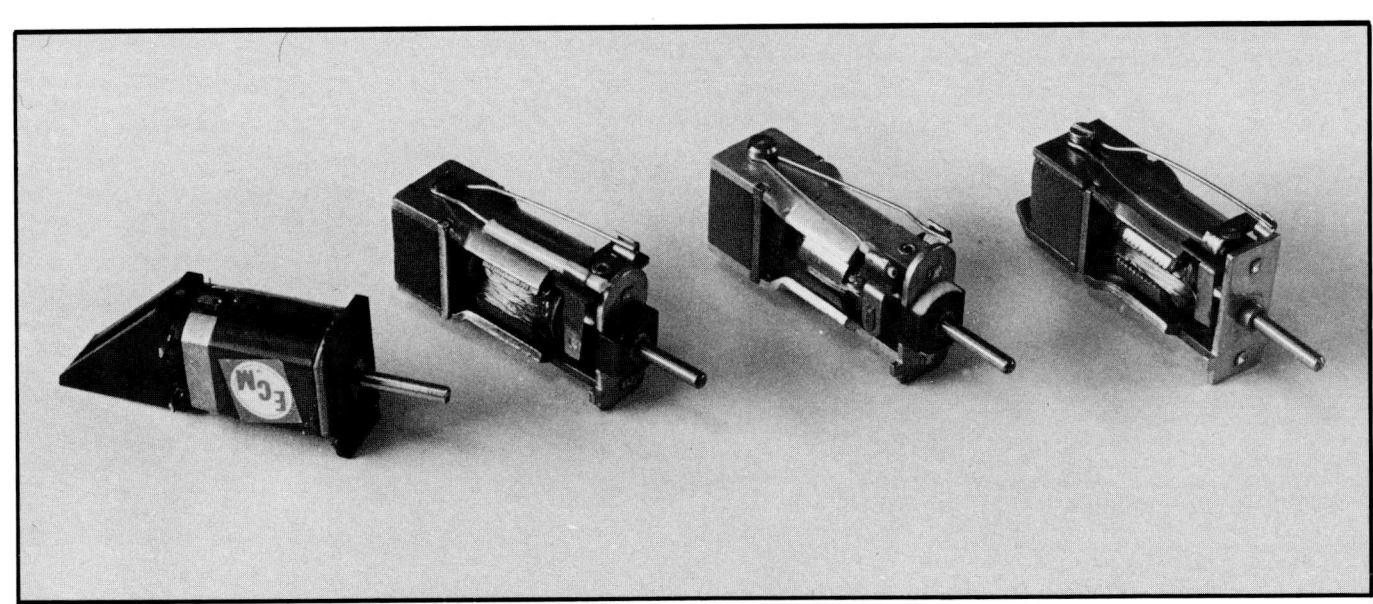

*Left:* **A Kean Portescap RG4 motor and gearbox supplied as a complete unit.**

*Below:* **The completed chassis for the Drewry shunting locomotive fitted with Portescap motor and gearbox.** *S. W. Stevens-Stratten*

*Bottom:* **The underside view of the Drewry chassis showing the pick-up connections and the gears.** *S. W. Stevens-Stratten*

coupling or connecting rods are binding on the crankpin or the boss. Check this and although 'cheating' you may find that by slightly enlarging the hole in the coupling rod you will cure the problem.

The valve gear in most modern kits is usually in etched brass or nickel-silver. As always this must be removed from the sheet making certain that all burrs around the 'pips' are filed off. The parts should be laid out on a clean piece of paper (a dark coloured paper will show up the parts) remembering that there is a right- and left-hand side and that any fluting should be uppermost. The instruction sheet should give a diagram showing the assembly and this must be strictly followed. Usually the parts are riveted together, so place a rivet underneath the joint and through the holes provided in the rods or arms. The hollow end of the rivet should now be uppermost and this is 'peened' over with light taps from a small hammer (a 4oz is quite sufficient). Some people prefer to use a small punch over the rivet and hit the punch with the hammer rather than the hammer hitting the actual rivet. This is a matter of personal preference and whichever suits you best is the method to use. The riveted joint should be perfectly free and must not be tight or give any friction in its movement.

At all stages of riveting, make certain that the parts will move freely. One idea used by some scratchbuilders is to place a small piece of good quality writing paper between the various rods when riveting. In this way when the paper is removed there will be just sufficient play, and it can save troubles if the rivet is accidently hammered too tightly.

The piston rod and crosshead are made up in accordance with the instructions again taking care that the sliding fit is perfectly free.

The diagram of the Walschaerts valve gear in this chapter should assist the kit-builder to identify the various parts and their location to each other.

The cylinders and their sub-assembly must now be made up for attaching to the chassis. With a cast kit this is no problem, but with an etched kit it will probably mean that the cylinders have to be formed from flat sheet. When the parts are ready they should be bent round a suitable object to get the rough shape, and then soldered together and to the cylinder covers, etc.

Some kits provide a motor with a worm already fitted to the shaft, but more often than not this has to be fitted by the builder. Fitting the worm is easy enough once it has been established it is in the right position. It can be fixed with adhesive, it can be soldered, or you may find that it has a grub screw for tightening to the shaft. If this is the

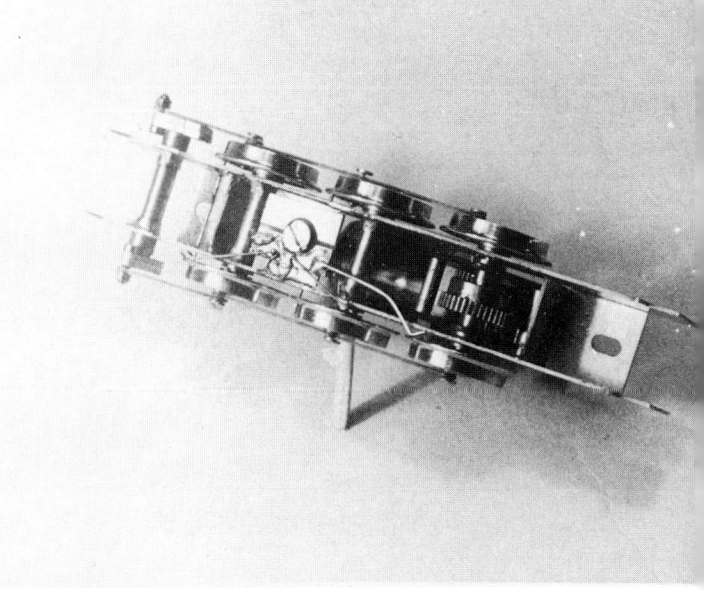

case it is still best to apply a small quantity of adhesive just to prevent it from turning on the shaft if the screw becomes loose. The best adhesive is one of the Super Glue brands and only a little is required as it will creep under the worm by capillary action. If you are soldering be careful you do not have too much heat and damage the motor. It is a good idea to use a small D clamp screwed to the armature shaft right up close to the motor (if there is room for it and the worm). This clamp will then act as a heat sink, taking the heat away from the shaft at this point. Now tin the axle and when cool smear a little Fluxite on this and also on the female hole in the worm. Slide the worm on to the shaft and apply a little heat and a little solder at the end of the worm.

With the motor temporarily wedged or fixed in place try the meshing of the gears for free running. The teeth should engage freely and be neither too tight nor too sloppy. Make adjustments to the position or rake of the motor on its mounting to correct either way and continue until you can turn the armature freely by hand which in turn should slowly turn the wheels. Fix the motor down and attach power leads to ensure that it will run freely and no further adjustment should have to be made.

The electrical pick-up from the insulated wheels (the ones on the right-hand side) can now be fixed. Pick-ups vary but are generally of phosphor bronze or some other 'springy' wire with good conductivity. They are bent to just touch the rear of the wheel rim, or the tyre or tread at the top just under the footplate where it will not show. The wire is generally attached to a piece of Paxolin or other suitable insulated material which is fixed across the frames and from here a thin wire is taken to the motor terminal via the shortest route. It is important to ensure that it will not foul the motion or the wheels and that it will not get trapped or squeezed when the body is in position. Soldering is essential for these connections. The more pick-ups there are the smoother the running, especially if the trackwork has the dead-frog type of points. Pick-ups should therefore be on all the driving wheels on one side, and if you are building a four-coupled tender loco it is a good idea also to have pick-ups on the tender wheels and connect this to the loco by a wire. This has the disadvantage that the loco must be permanently coupled to the tender, although there are some very small plugs and sockets available on the market.

The chassis should now be given another good run to make certain that everything is perfect. It will benefit from a prolonged run and it will be beneficial if this can be carried out on a continuous test track, changing the direction after 20 minutes or so. Check that the motor is not running hot and that there are no extraneous noises coming from the gears, or valve gear. If no track is available the loco can be put on blocks or into a cradle upside down and leads from the controller attached to the pick-ups or direct to the motor. The chassis can then be run at half-speed for 40 minutes or so, again changing direction half way through the test.

The motor bearings, axle bearings, and gears should all have a drop of oil, but not too much. The oil should be a good quality light sewing-machine oil, but beware that you do not use any oil which the makers claim 'will free rusty bolts' as these can attack plastic and in all probability the wheel centres and hubs will be some form of plastic. The oil should be applied with a wire so that just a small drop is put exactly where it is required.

When the testing is complete the chassis should be put aside in a box to keep it from dust until the body has been painted and the two parts can be permanently united.

*Top:* **A typical chassis with brass frames and XO4 type motor. It was designed to fit the Wills kit of the LMSR 'Flatiron' 0-6-4T.**

*Below:* **A 0-4-4 chassis with motor at an angle and fixed in position by screw adjustment on the right hand side, above the bogie wheels. The chassis is a solid block of cast metal, the axle holes having brass bearings. It is designed to fit the Wills 'M7' body kit.**

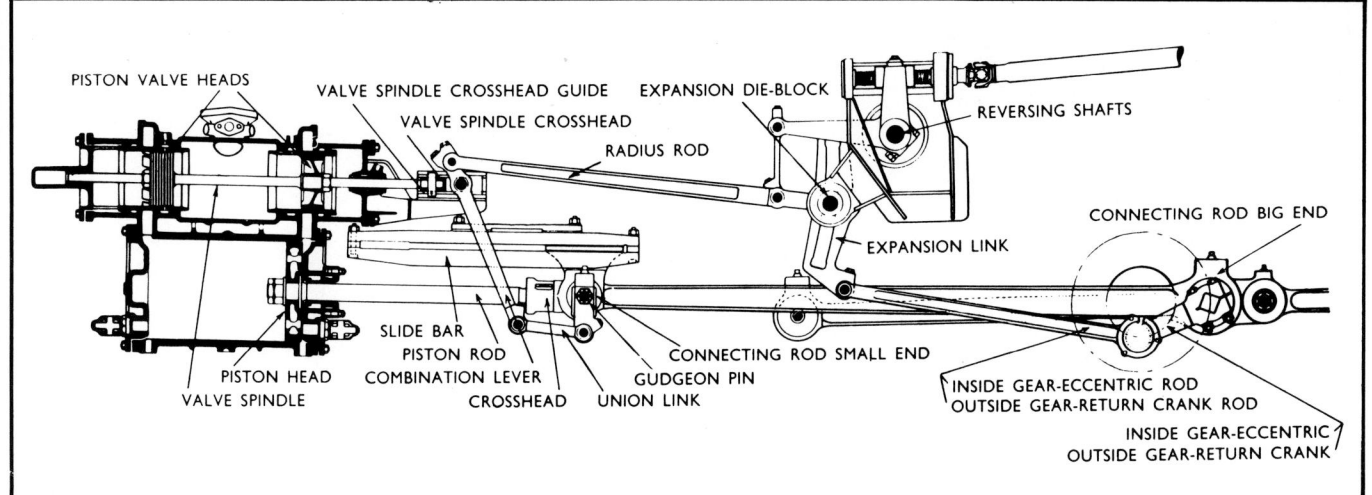

*Above:* **Diagram showing the position and names of parts for Walschaerts valve gear.**

*Below:* **Diagram showing the position and names of parts for Stephenson valve gear.**

*Bottom:* **Diagram showing the position and names of parts for British Caprotti valve gear.**

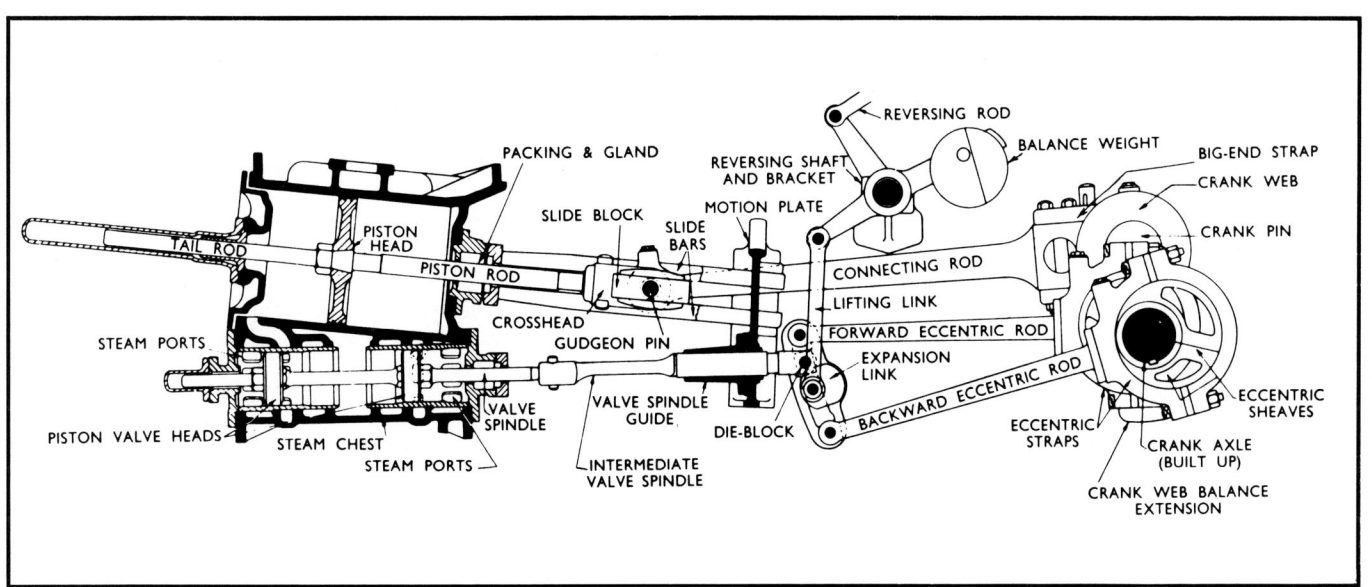

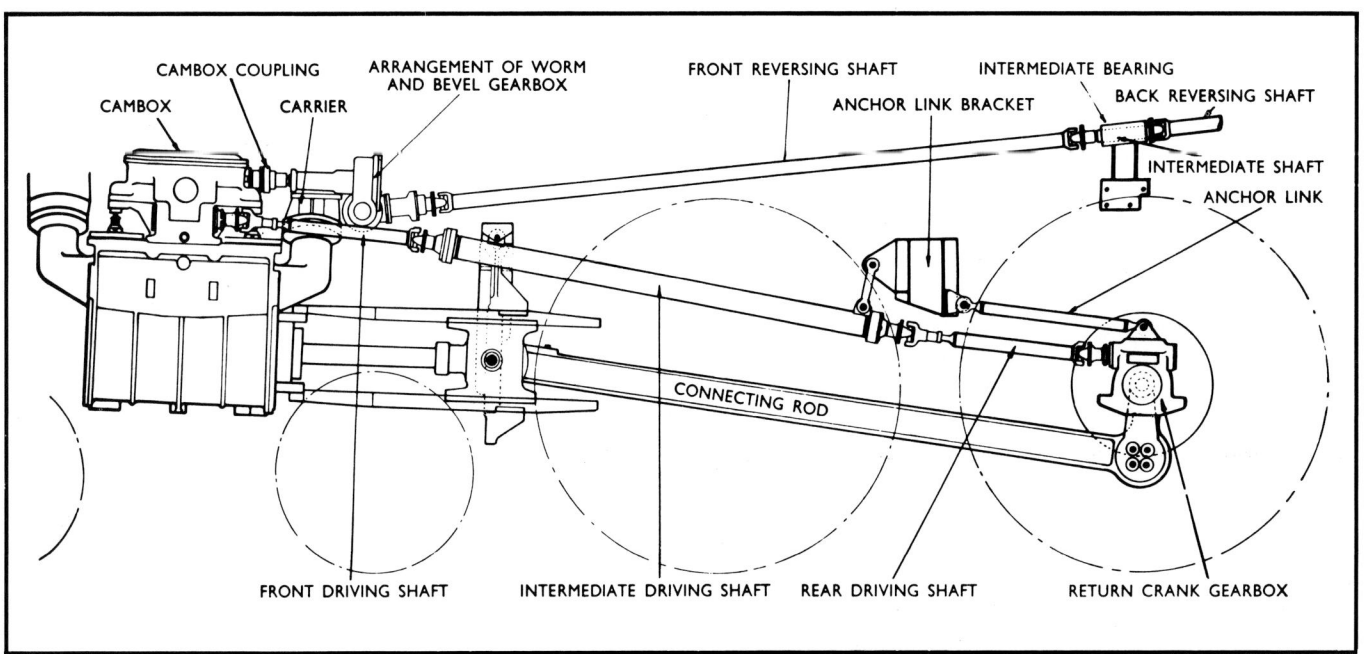

# Painting

When the assembly has been completed the model is ready for painting and it is true to say that more good models have been spoilt by bad painting than anything else. As already stated it is prudent to paint during the assembly some of the parts which are in the completed model partly inaccessible and these include the chassis sides and the wheels, plus any other parts which the design of the kit or prototype may determine — the inside face of any smoke deflectors being an example.

Assuming that all cracks have been filled and any excess of solder or adhesive has been removed, the next step is to polish gently any rough surfaces with a wire brush. One of the best types is the kind sold for cleaning suede shoes, but a glass fibre brush used lightly is also effective.

The most important step before any paint is applied is to wash the model thoroughly. This will remove not only dirt and grease which can accumulate on the surface, but also get rid of the residue of any flux (of whatever variety) which may be trapped in crevices or even lying along an exposed joint. Failure to remove the residue of some fluxes will cause blisters and marks to appear in the paintwork at a later stage. The washing is best done with warm water, a household detergent such as washing-up liquid and a small scrubbing brush — an old toothbrush is ideal for this purpose.

When the thorough washing of all parts, except of course the motor, has been completed the model should be put in a warm place to dry. Do not attempt to hasten the drying process by putting the model in an oven or on top of a radiator as too fierce a heat can be detrimental to castings and joints. One of the upper shelves of an airing cupboard is ideal, or you can even get sufficient heat by placing the model a foot above a 60W electric light bulb for an hour or so. A gentle warmth for a few hours is all that is required, and a warm room overnight is just as good.

Do not touch the model with your bare hands if you can avoid it, for it is surprising how much natural oiliness there can be in the human skin — some people more than others.

The model should now receive a coat of primer. One of the best types is a cellulose primer in an aerosol can which is marketed for the motor car DIY trade. Available from most car accessory shops and garages for about £1 (price at time of writing) the can will prime about six or eight medium size 4mm scale model locomotives. The can should be well shaken and used as per the instructions printed thereon. Even passes of the can over the model, which should be resting on an old piece of cardboard or wood so that it can be rotated, will ensure an even coat of paint. This operation can be carried out in the open, but if indoors it should be done inside an open box as shown in one of the illustrations, otherwise the excess spray will get everywhere. Also make certain that the job is undertaken in a well ventilated room and away from any naked flame or electric or gas radiators of the exposed type.

Primer may also be brushed on and several firms who supply model railway paints also market a primer. The problem with brushing is that however careful you are a brush mark or even a 'run' can quickly occur and unless this is eradicated immediately it will show through the finishing coats unless rubbed down well. Again it is not so easy to get down into some of the obscure places which the spray will penetrate easily.

The primer may, of course, be used with an airbrush or small spray gun, but by the time the airbrush or gun has been connected and it has been thoroughly cleaned afterwards, you will find it quicker and more economical to use one of the aerosol cans as suggested. Further some of the primer paints have a form of etching solution in them to make them adhere and this can cause damage to the fine needle of an airbrush over a period of time.

At this stage you have to worry about the livery of your model. You presumably have already decided on the actual period you have in mind to depict and this may well predetermine the livery. This is particularly true for a diesel loco on BR where pre-1967/68 the livery was two shades of green and since that date is Rail blue. It is not within the scope of this book to give full lists of all the liveries and lining colours for all the various railway companies for this is an exhaustive subject in itself. It is therefore recommended that you obtain the information from other books and you should already have photographs of the prototype you are modelling. This will show you where the lining goes, the position of nameplates, number plates etc. A good introduction to the subject can be found in Ian Allan's 'Railway Liveries' series by Brian Haresnape.

*Below left:* **A Humbrol spray gun with compressed air canister.**

*Below:* **A Compton small and portable compressor coupled to a Humbrol Airbrush.**

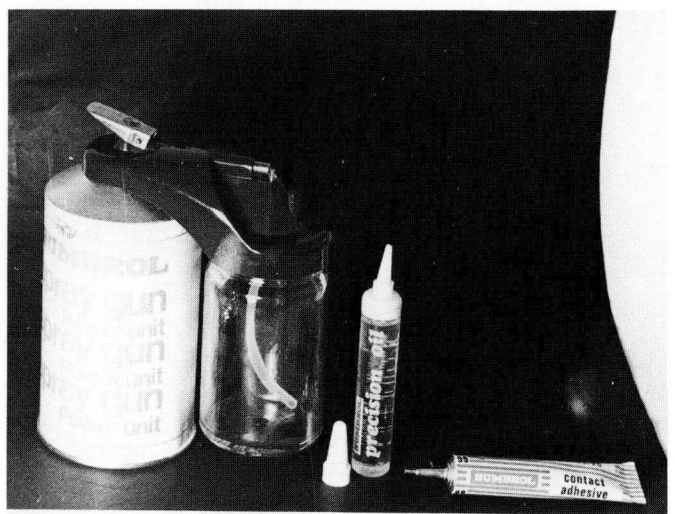

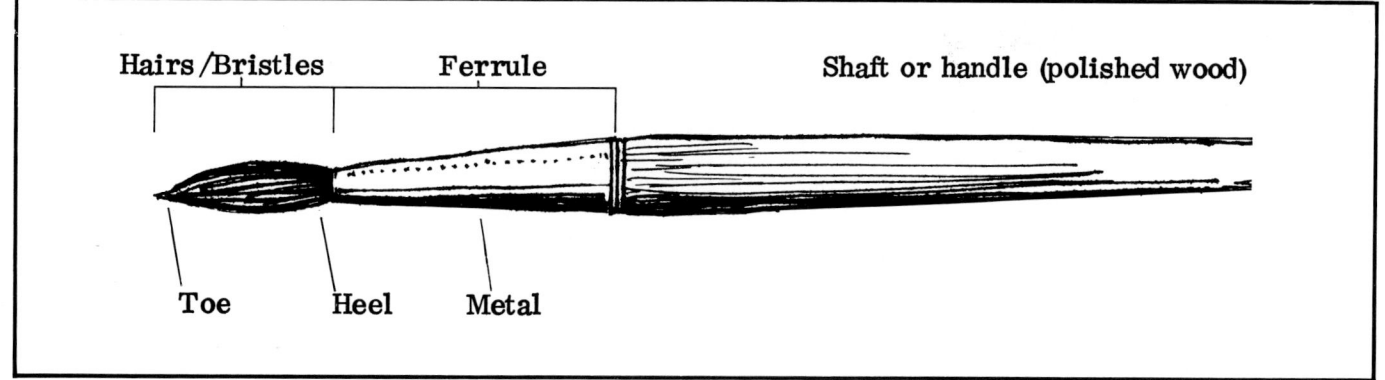

*Above:* **Paint brushes should have a good tip (or toe), and it will be beneficial to buy brushes of good quality.**

*Left:* **The three popular types of bristle shapes for paintbrushes needed for modelling.**

*Below:* **Common faults in brushes caused by neglect, but mainly bad storage.**

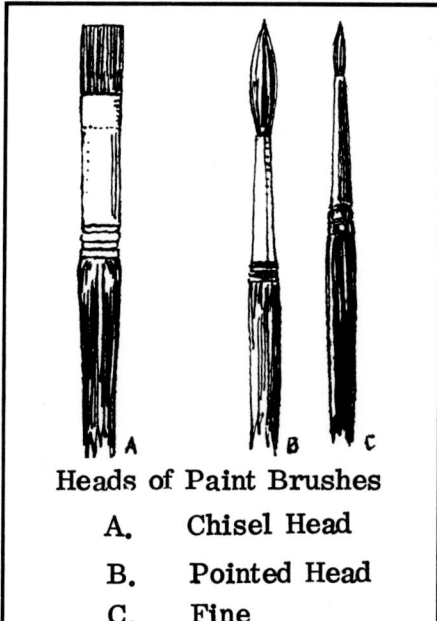

Heads of Paint Brushes
A. Chisel Head
B. Pointed Head
C. Fine

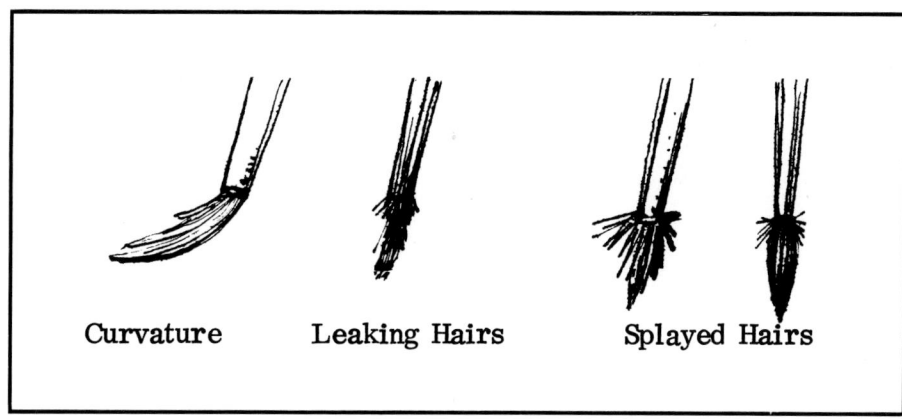

Curvature  Leaking Hairs  Splayed Hairs

Having decided on the livery you now have to get the paint. There are several makes of authentic railway colours on the market — Humbrol, Precision Paint and Compucolour being the best known. There are some others, including the American made Floquil and Scalecoat ranges, which are xylene based and although very good, they have a most obnoxious smell and the fumes when sprayed may be toxic. There is also Polly-S which is water soluble and particularly useful for plastics.

Cellulose paint is ideal, but is not available in railway colours: although aerosol cans for use with motor cars come in a variety of colours, few are a proper match. If the loco is to be painted plain black then a matt black can be obtained in this range and can be recommended. Cellulose paints should not be used on plastics.

When purchasing the paint do not forget to obtain the appropriate thinners. While ordinary White Spirit (synthetic turpentine) can be used for some paints, it is not as effective as the proper thinners for that particular brand of paint.

The paint should be of the eggshell or semi-matt finish. Flat matt is too flat when it dries and a high gloss looks most unrealistic.

Before you start to paint there are a few general hints which should be borne in mind: Never rush the job; have all you need ready to hand, be relaxed and take your time. Never try to economise on paint. Never try to put one thick coat on instead of two thin ones, or the finished result will look as if you used a tar-brush or the kitchen washing-up mop!

The painting area should be as free from dust as possible, not only while you are painting, but especially while the model is drying. Never try to put a second coat on the model until the first coat is really hard, and manufacturer's drying times should be doubled — just to be on the safe side. Never put a cellulose based paint on top of an oil based one — and caution is advised if the former is put straight on to some plastics, as it may result in an unwanted 'crackle enamel' finish. It is advisable to use a clear barrier solution as sold under the Floquil banner if this paint is to be used on plastics.

All paints must be stirred thoroughly and one of the best ways to do this is to unbend one side of a paper clip and place this in the chuck of a small electric mini-drill, using this as a mixer. Do not use a power drill — unless you want paint everywhere but in the tin! The importance of correctly mixed or stirred paint cannot be over-emphasised not only for the true rendering of the colour it is supposed to represent, but also to ensure that the varnish in the paint is correctly mixed. One make of semi-matt paint will dry to a glossy finish unless it is thoroughly stirred, and it will also take several days to dry. Tins of paint are easier to mix if they have been stored lid downwards (providing the lid is a good fit) which also prevents a skin from forming.

There are two methods of applying the paint — by brush or by spraying — and we will deal with each in turn.

*Brushing*

It is false economy to buy cheap brushes and the sable haired ones, although expensive, will last a long time, if looked after carefully. A No 2 for fine lines and a No 4 for general use are recommended. The author likes the chisel shaped variety as they seem to given an even coating with less likelihood of brush marks. All brushes should be kept scrupulously clean in a screw stoppered jar or tube with the hairs uppermost, so they are not squashed or bent. When you have finished with a brush, wash it thoroughly in clean thinners and rinse out with soap and water. A little white spirit poured in a small jar or bottle (fish paste jar or ink bottle is ideal) to start with and when all the paint is out, transfer to another bottle with a little clean thinners. If you are economically minded the first bottle can be used again for

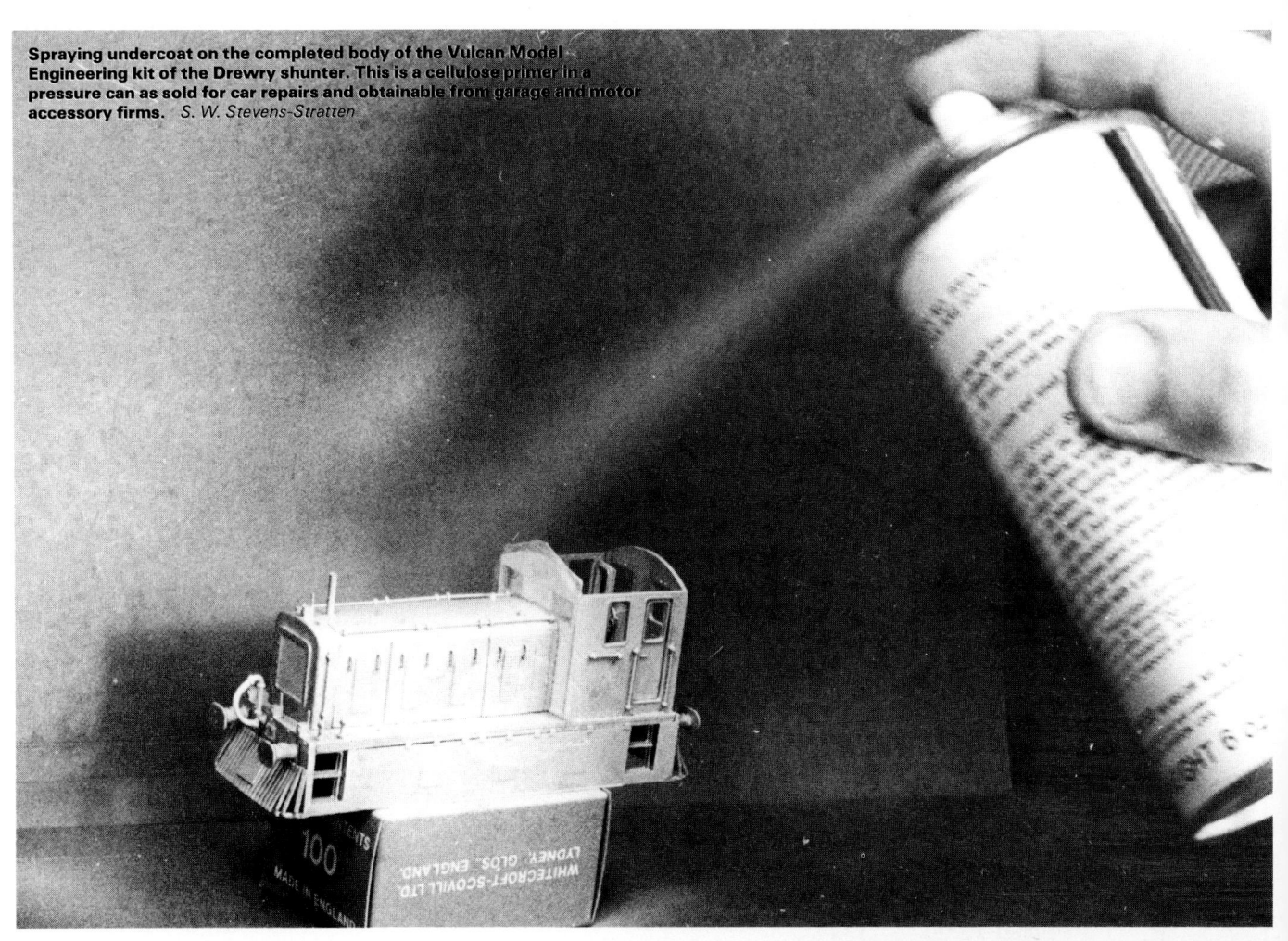

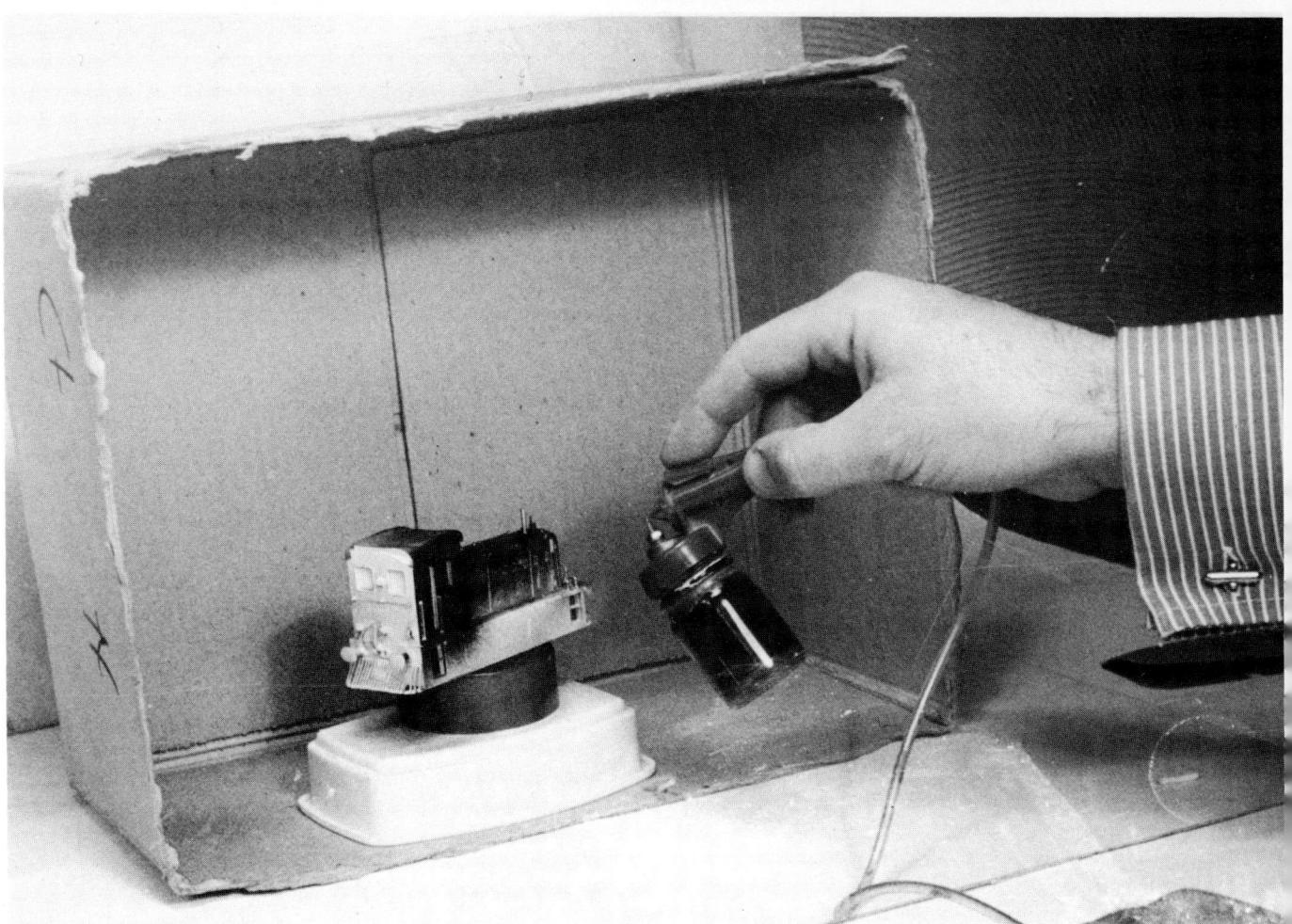

**Spraying undercoat on the completed body of the Vulcan Model Engineering kit of the Drewry shunter. This is a cellulose primer in a pressure can as sold for car repairs and obtainable from garage and motor accessory firms.** *S. W. Stevens-Stratten*

an initial brush wash, providing it is followed by a clean one. Yet another bottle with a little washing-up liquid in warm water can be used to give the brush a final rinse. Make certain that all the paint is out of the top end of the bristles (called the ferrule). The brush should now be dried on a lint-free cloth and placed in a dust free atmosphere to dry thoroughly. When dry, it should be returned to its jar or stoppered tube and stored hair uppermost.

When brush painting, the paint should be thinned slightly if necessary and the brush dipped into the paint with not more than half its bristles getting covered. Use the brush lightly on the model so that the bristles are just bending backwards. Use long strokes, moving in one direction only. The exception is at the point where there is raised detail such as boiler bands. If the brush is kept in one direction — ie at 90deg to the boiler band — this will have the effect of dragging extra paint off the brush and this will tend to run at the side of the projection and therefore be thicker at this location. This can be overcome by running the brush downwards alongside the boiler band before commencing the horizontal strokes and then feathering the paint in.

Make certain the paint is not being put on the model too thickly, as it will then run, particularly round the boiler — nothing is more annoying than to find the paint drying out with runs appearing in the middle of a nice smooth surface.

For best results put the model on a clean piece of old wood or cardboard so that it can be turned without being touched. Make certain that your hand and wrist are quite comfortable and can move freely.

When the model has been covered with a thin film of paint, put it on one side to dry. It is a good idea to put some form of cover over the model such as a box, but put some blocks of wood at the corners so that air can get underneath and help the drying process. Remember most of the dust falls on the model from above, so keep it covered.

When the paint is thoroughly dry and hard, it can then be given a second coat. If you try to put this on too soon, you will find that the second coat is trying to lift the first coat of paint.

For the best results you cannot beat an airbrush or a small spray gun, which are expensive but are worth their weight in gold if you are an enthusiast and likely to build more kits. They are also useful for painting other things like scenery. The airbrush will spray out a fine mist which will give an even and thin coating of paint which will dry quickly. Other advantages are that a professional finish can easily be obtained, you can control the amount of paint being delivered, overspray is virtually non-existent as a very fine line can be sprayed if desired (although masking is required for a really sharp edge). Applying a second coat does not pull off the first, as so often happens with brushing, and there is no build-up of paint at edges. Shades can be blended from thick to thin at the turn of a knob, which is marvellous for scenic work or for 'weathering' effects on locomotives and rolling stock. With an airbrush the spraying of gold, silver or other metallic paints gives a superlative result which is unequalled by other means.

There are two popular forms of air supply (or propulsion) for the airbrush — the propellant aerosol canister or a compressor. A car tyre can be used but is not recommended as it bulky and it needs a pressure of 35-40lb/sq in which can be quite dangerous for some old tyres that may explode if well worn or weak. Furthermore, because the tyre deflates rapidly, while there will be enough pressure to undertake the first coat, it is doubtful whether there is enough 'punch' to clean the airbrush and put on a second coat.

A CO2 cylinder is quite good and refills are cheap, but the initial cost is high, as are hire charges, and within a couple of years the money spent would go a long way towards buying a compressor.

The aerosol can is small, neat, clean and portable and seems to keep its pressure fairly constant until towards the very end of its life. Cans vary in size from 10oz to 30oz and are connected directly to the airline of the spray gun or airbrush. Prices vary but at the time of writing are approximately £1.50. It is a good idea to stand the tin in a bowl of water at room temperature, because the canister will frost on the outside. This is the same effect as absorption refrigerators where the gas takes in the difference of the ambient temperature. The can must always be kept upright.

The ultimate power supply for spraying (either airbrush or gun) is a compressor, and although the initial price is high, it is a lot less in the long run than you will spend on frequent purchases of aerosol cans or CO2 cylinders, especially if the airbrush is used fairly regularly. The main advantage of the compressor is a continual flow of air at the pressure specified — many compressors having an adjustable output valve.

Paints for spraying have to be thinned and as a rough approximation — it obviously depends on the viscosity of the paint in the first place — use just a little less than one third thinners for three parts of the usual Humbrol paint until it is about the consistency of milk. If the paint is too thin it will run on the model and will not cover well, but if it is too thick it will 'splatter' and build up on the nozzle of the brush. The paint must also be thoroughly mixed, not with a piece of wire but with a spatula or something similar. A flat bit of Plastikard or one of the BR so-called 'tea-stirrers' are ideal.

The model should now be placed in the improvised spray booth, as for priming, the paint should be well stirred and connected to the airbrush, which in turn is connected to the propellant; then, a quick burst on an odd scrap of wood or metal to ensure that the paint is running through correctly, and we are ready.

At this stage it is assumed that you have already tried out the airbrush and are familiar with its action and what it can do. If not, practice using a bottle of blue or black ink. This is cheap, works well and it will enable you to control the brush from a large area down to a fine line. Try writing your initials on a piece of paper or card! It can be done quite easily with practice. The beauty of using ordinary ink — apart from relative cheapness — is that when you have finished you merely spray water through the system and it quickly cleans the brush.

The technique for spraying is simple and all spray guns include an instruction book with hints and tips. Keep the correct distance from the object being sprayed — you'll soon get used to this — and keep the wrist straight, moving the arm horizontally along the length of the model. Keep the airbrush moving and do not keep it in one place. It is important that you do not bend your wrist, keep it perfectly straight so that the airbrush nozzle is always at right angles to the model. Start spraying just before the model so that the full blast of paint is carried on to the front of the model, and not just the opening spurts.

It is unusual that a locomotive would need masking anywhere, except perhaps the bufferbeam, or if you have foolishly added the cab windows before painting. If this is the case, mask the parts not needing paint (or to be painted a different colour at a later stage) with masking tape. Ordinary Sellotape can be used, but because of its tenacious nature it may pull off any paint underneath and it can also mark windows or glazing material. The proper masking tape has 'low-tack' properties and is easily removable. You can also use one of the liquid masking agents such as Humbrol Maskol, which is a type of liquid rubber which dries solid immediately after painting on and can be peeled off afterwards.

Cleaning the airbrush or spray gun is simplicity itself. Merely remove the paint container and replace with one containing white spirit or thinners. Spray through for a few seconds until pure and clean spirits appears on the old bit of material you are aiming at. Remove the container and wipe the outside of the brush with a piece of lint-free cloth. Naturally you must clean the paint container in the normal manner.

*Left:* **Airbrushing the final coat on the Drewry shunter. Note the model has been placed on an improvised pedestal so it can be turned without touching the actual model and it is being sprayed into an old open box to save the spray from getting on to the table and walls etc.**
*S. W. Stevens-Stratten*

*Right:* **A typical sheet of transfers giving many variations and sizes of the prototype lettering. These are the water-slide type produced by SMS Model Supplies.**

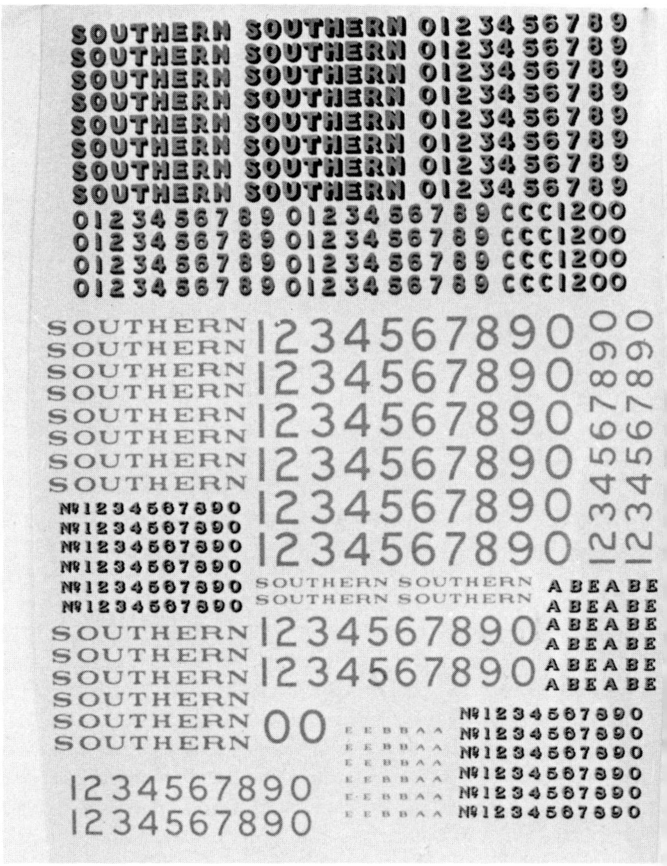

*Below:* **The completed 4mm scale model of the Vulcan Model Engineering kit of the BR Drewry shunter.**

*Bottom:* **A well cleaned body ready to receive a coat of priming paint.**

# Lining and Lettering

There are no short cuts for either lining or lettering and you are left with a choice of either using transfers or undertaking the work by hand. Obviously transfers of the rub-on or waterslide types are easier, but even then there are plenty of pitfalls to trap the unwary.

**Transfers**

Fortunately there are a number of dry print sheets on the market for the model railway enthusiast and Kingsprint and some Letraset sheets can give good results, providing the manufacturers' instructions are followed. Try and keep the sheets in an air-tight container as we have found that old sheets can give trouble in releasing the transfer or line. Difficulty is usually experienced in getting the lining round the boiler bands, as naturally you are not working on a flat surface. Some modellers will release the lining on to a piece of glass and then lift it and reposition it on its proper location, but this is not always easy to accomplish. Another problem can be encountered when rubbing the lining strips on curves, such as dropped footplates or wheel splashers. Only practice on these intricate shapes can make perfect.

The lettering and numbering is, of course, quite an easy matter and very good results can be obtained with the dry print type of transfer, but remember to get it positioned absolutely right as it cannot be moved afterwards. The lining, letters and numbers should receive a light coat of matt varnish after they have been applied and should not be touched until the varnish has been put on. After the treatment they are more or less permanent.

Waterslide transfers are also relatively easy to apply, but these usually show a small area of transparent film around the edges: this is the carrier. A wide range of waterslide transfers are available from most good model shops or by mail order from the manufacturers and the range covers locos and rolling stock crests, letters and numbers from the pre-Grouping Companies up to the present day BR. All waterslide transfers have the advantage that they can be moved as applied so that correct positioning can be obtained. A variation on the waterslide transfer is the Methfix type manufactured by P C Models. Here the transfers are applied with a dilution of methylated spirit and water and leave no carrier film.

A cross between the rub-on type and the waterslide transfer is the Pressfix range, also from P C Models. Here the transfer is pressed down on to the model, and then the backing sheet is removed by an application of water.

When all is finished the transfers should have a coat of matt varnish to protect them from lifting, but wait until all traces of moisture has evaporated and make certain that they are flat with no air bubbles underneath. It is safest to leave for a day before varnishing, and only a thin coat should be applied. Letraset makes a matt varnish in an aerosol spray can and this can be most useful for our purpose.

The older type of varnish fixing transfer have now become outdated and difficult to obtain. They were always difficult to apply and have now been superseded by the waterslide type.

**Hand Lining and Lettering**

The other method of applying lining is by hand with either a bow pen or a very fine brush. The latter is really an artist's job and as few people have the skill to undertake brush work of such an intricate and detailed nature, the bow pen is much preferred.

The bow pen is not as difficult as it may seem and like many things it is a case of 'practice makes perfect'. Obtain a good quality bow pen and practise on odd scraps of metal or plastic until you are confident that you know exactly what it can do — and what you can do! The width of the line to be painted is determined by the size of the opening of the 'jaws' of the pen and adjusted by the knurled nut on the side. The paint is best put into the gap between the jaws with a brush, but it must be of the right consistency — something like single cream is ideal. If you have the paint too thin it will spread and if it is too thick it will not come out of the pen. Never overload the pen, about $\frac{1}{4}$in up the 'jaws' is about right. Use an oil or acrylic paint which can be wiped off immediately if you make a mistake and there is less risk of damaging the previously painted surface. A good tip is to add a little soapy water in the paint mixture as this will help it flow and adhere to the surface. Using a ruler as a guide line, practise first on odd scraps of metal or plastic until you are fully conversant with its use. Never overload the pen, keep it clean and wipe it free of congealing paint every few minutes. Don't let paint get on the outside of the jaws.

While you are doing the lettering and lining, it is a good idea to put the locomotive in a cradle, which will hold it fast, and use a block of wood — or similar — to steady your painting hand (see illustration). An alternative method of making lining — particularly boiler bands — is to paint very narrow lines on cigarette papers. (Rizla 'Red' for handmade 'roll-ups'!)

When the paint is dry, the paper can be placed on a sheet of glass (held at each end with Sellotape) and then cut into thin strips with a rule and a craft knife. The resultant strips can then be stuck on to the model with a very thin film of varnish — but the whole operation is easier said than done! Again you will have to have a thin film of varnish on top of paper when the underneath is dry.

Remember never work in a hurry, allow plenty of time and try to be relaxed.

*Below:* **A Wills kit of the SE&CR Class C 0-6-0 in pre-Grouping livery with full lining.**

# Finishing Touches

Your model is now complete with the exception of those little pieces of detail which have to be fixed on after the painting. These include the glazing of cab windows and the fixing of name and number plates etc. These items are best fixed with a spot of adhesive, but not so much that it oozes out from under the item being put on! Cab windows can be fixed with Evo-Stik but make certain it does not string and make a mark across the glazing. It is best to apply a very thin film around the inside of the aperture and the edge of the glazing material, and wait until it is really 'tacky' — say about 10 or 15min, and then carefully place the glazing in position. This has to be done right first time as it will really stick hard.

Scale lamps, usually cast metal, can be obtained, painted white and placed on the bufferbeam, which should of course be painted red.

Coal or imitation coal should be glued into the tender. Real coal, if you can obtain this, can be crushed down to scale size lumps, or a packet of scenic coal can be purchased from a good model shop. For the adhesive we recommend either Evo-Stik or white PVA adhesive. If you use Evo-Stik, you coat the tender coal plate with the adhesive and then press in the coal; if you use the white PVA adhesive (at a 1:1 dilution with water) you put the coal in the tender first and then drop on the glue with an eye dropper — it dries transparent.

*Below:* **A K's kit of the GWR 55xx 2-6-2T which are known as the 'small prairie' tanks. The kit has added detail such as headlamp brackets etc and is fitted with Romford driving and pony wheels and powered by a MW005 motor. The model was constructed by Alan Ketley.** *Trevor Baily*

# Some Completed Kits

*Above and below:* **A Nu-Cast Model Engineering kit for a GWR 16xx class 0-6-0PT. This kit was originally produced by Cotswold Models. Even an opening smokebox can be constructed to show the flues etc as shown.**

*Right:* **Caledonian Railway Class 60 depicted in LMSR livery is a DJH 4mm scale kit.**

*Below far right:* **A 7mm scale kit of a 0-4-0ST 'Pug' which has fully detailed cab fittings by Sevenscale.**

*Below:* **A 4mm scale Southern Railway Class M7 0-4-4T by Wills.**

41

*Right:* **This M&L (Model & Leisure) 4mm scale kit of the GWR Class 1076 0-6-0ST has an etched brass chassis and cast metal body.**

*Below:* **An N gauge locomotive kit from Langley Miniature Models. A GWR 56xx class 0-6-2T.**

*Below centre:* **A McGowan kit of Furness Railway 0-6-2T in 4mm scale.**

*Bottom:* **A DJH cast kit of an ex-LB&SCR Class C2X painted in BR black livery.**

# Completed Kits in their Natural Surroundings

*Left:* **A 4mm scale, P4 gauge model of a Robert Stephenson Hawthorns 0-4-0ST on the 'Preesgwyn' layout of Paul Gittins. The locomotive body is a Centre Models kit with scratchbuilt chassis.** *Brian Monaghan*

*Below:* **This model of a 14xx class GWR 0-4-2T is again on the same layout of Paul Gittins. The body is a K's kit on a scratchbuilt compensated chassis fitted with Mike Sharman wheels and a Anchoridge DS10 motor and Romford 40:1 gears.** *Brian Monaghan*

*Above right:* **A Bec 4mm scale kit of the SR Class D16 running on the 'Gallows Hill and Tyburn' layout of Ian Scott. Romford wheels are fitted to the locomotive.** *Brian Monaghan*

*Right:* **A GEM kit of an ex-LNWR 0-8-0 built by John Porter on the EM gauge layout of Bill Pearce. It looks as if the locomotive has slightly over-run the signal!** *Brian Monaghan*

*Below:* **A modification to represent an auto-fitted model of a Cotswold (now Nu-Cast) kit of a L&YR 2-4-2T built by John porter for the above layout.** *Brian Monaghan*

*Left:* **No 6832** *Brockton Grange* **hauls a freight over a bridge on the 4mm scale North Devonshire layout of Ken Northwood. The locomotive is a K's kit with added detail, and the motor in the tender drives the loco wheels via a universal jointed shaft.** *Brian Monaghan*

*Below left:* **Another K's kit on the same layout. This time a model of 43xx class 2-6-0. It is fitted with a Pitman DD195 motor and 41:1 gears.** *Brian Monaghan*

*Below:* **An ex-MR Johnstone 2-4-0 crosses a bridge on the P4 gauge 'Port Dinlleyn' layout of the Blackburn & East Lancs MRS. The body of the loco is a Ratio plastic kit. The chassis is handbuilt with a 'can' type motor in the tender.** *Brian Monaghan*

*Bottom:* **Another view of the same layout, this time the LNWR 4-4-2T has a GEM white metal kit body and scratchbuilt chassis for P4 standards.** *Brian Monaghan*

*Below:* **A Wills kit of a GWR Metro tank (2-4-0T) pulls into a station on the 'Buxton Road' 4mm scale layout of T. A. Quinn. The Wills chassis is fitted with a 5 pole MW motor and 40:1 gears.** *Brian Monaghan*

## PERSEVERANCE

### VARIFLEX LOCO CHASSIS KITS

A range of loco & tender chassis kits to really bring out the best in your ready to run and kit built models. Based on Mike Sharman's flexichas principle, a fully compensated chassis giving much better looks, improved traction for better hauling power, better current collection and much finer control, especially at low speeds. The kits are designed to be very easy to build, even for the absolute beginner, and fully detailed instructions are given.

Kits contain mainframes, brake gear, coupling rods, spring detail, frame spacers for OO, EM and 18.83 gauges, all bearings etc (where applicable bogie units and cylinders, valve gears etc).

| | |
|---|---|
| LNER J72 0-6-0T ............... £8.00 | GWR County 4-6-0 ............. £13.45 |
| LNER N2 0-6-2T ............... £10.20 | GWR Manor 4-6-0 ............. £12.95 |
| GWR 57xx 0-6-0 Pannier ......... £8.50 | GWR 94xx 0-6-0 Pannier ......... £8.50 |
| GWR 14xx 0-4-2T (& 517 class) .. £8.50 | GWR City, Flower, Atbara 4-4-0 £11.95 |
| GWR 2251 Collett Goods 0-6-0 ... £8.50 | GWR Duke, Bulldog 4-4-0 ...... £11.50 |
| GWR Dean Goods 0-6-0 .......... £8.50 | LMS Fowler 4F 0-6-0 ........... £8.50 |
| GWR Castle (4073-4092) ........ £12.95 | LMS Jinty 0-6-0T ............... £8.50 |
| GWR Castle (4093-7037) ........ £12.95 | GWR Tender chassis ............ £6.00 |
| GWR Star 4-6-0 ............... £12.95 | GWR tender for 4 coupled locos .. £7.50 |
| GWR Saint 4-6-0 .............. £13.45 | LMS Fowler tender ............. £6.00 |
| GWR Hall 4-6-0 ............... £13.45 | LMS tender for 4 coupled locos ... £7.50 |

FULL RANGE OF HORNBLOCKS etc FOR CONVERTING ANY KIT CHASSIS TO THE VARIFLEX SYSTEM IS AVAILABLE, eg for an 0-6-0 would cost just **£1.75**. 1984 ILLUSTRATED PERSEVERANCE CATALOGUE, **75p+17p** stamp. Hundreds of useful items & tools for the kit builder.

**PERSEVERANCE MODEL RAILWAYS,
MALVERN HOUSE, MALVERN ROAD,
CHELTENHAM GL50 2NU (Tel: 0242-30081).**

Mail order only. P&P maximum **60p**, over **£15** post free, Access & Barclaycard taken by phone.

## WESTWARD

### LOCOMOTIVE KITS, COACH KITS
and **BOGIES**, plus a large range of accessories for steam and diesel locos.

GWR 2800/3800 class 2-8-0 locomotive kit. Fully detailed white metal castings and etched chassis. Requires, wheels and Portescap motor. **£57.50** including VAT.

GWR Diesel Railcar No 18 white metal body kit to fit Lima Railcar chassis. **£26.45**.

GWR Coach Kits, diagram H39 + H40 restaurant cars. Etched brass sides, floor, white metal fittings. Bogies+wheels required to complete **£19.55** each.

*Full details of all our products in our current catalogue,* **50p** *including postage.*

**WESTWARD SCALE MODELS
CROW MEADOW, KINGSWOOD,
WOTTON-UNDER-EDGE, GLOUCESTER GL12 8RX**

*Tel: 04538 43338*      *Mail Order Only*

# Manufacturers

Listed below, under the applicable headings, is a list of firms who supply model locomotive kits and ancillary items. It is complete at the time of going to press but any errors or omissions must be accepted.

## Locomotive kits

*ABS* — (39 Napier Road, Hamworthy, Poole, Dorset). Mainly cast, 4mm, N and NG.
*Bristol Models* — (76 Station Road, Filton, Bristol). Mainly cast, 4mm. Etched chassis for other kits.
*Chivers Fineline* — (49 St Christines Avenue, Leyland, Preston). Mainly cast NG.
*Cotswold* — Now marketed by Nu-Sto.
*Goldspot* (formerly *DJH Models*)—(Consett, Co Durham). Cast 4mm.
*GEM* — (George E. Mellor, 31a Rhos Road, Rhos-on-Sea, Clwyd). Cast 4mm, N, TT and NG.
*Alan Gibson* — (The Bungalow, Church Road, Lingwood, Norwich, Norfolk). Cast and etched 4mm and 7mm.
*Jamieson/EAMES* — (24 Tudor Road, Reading or 14 York Way, King's Cross, London N1). Sheet metal 7mm.
*Jidenco Models* — (Well Cottage, 14 Claypits Lane, Shrivenham, Berks). Etched brass 4mm.
*K's* — (N. & K. C. Keyser Ltd, Grimsbury South Industrial Estate, Banbury, Oxon). Cast 4mm.
*Ian Kirk* — (14 East Street, St Monans, Fife). Cast 4mm NG.
*Langley Miniature Models* — (166 Three Bridges Road, Crawley, Sussex). Cast N (one cast 4mm).
*Leinster Models* — Sheet metal 7mm.
*Mallard Models* — Now discontinued.
*P. & D. Marsh* — Cast N.
*Model Loco Ltd* — (7B Cecil Street, Carlisle). Cast 4mm.
*Model & Leisure* — (101 Sewall Highway, Coventry). Cast 4mm.
*Modern Traction Kits* — Cast 4mm modern image.
*McGowan Models* — (7 Ringley Park Road, Reigate, Surrey). Cast 4mm.
*Nu-cast Kits* — (81 Clifton Avenue, Hartlepool, Cleveland). Cast 4mm.
*Q Kits* — Fibreglass 4mm modern image bodies.
*Ratio Plastic Models Ltd* — (Butts Pond, Sturminster Newton, Dorset). Plastic 4mm
*TMD* — (98 Parnell Road, Dolphins Barn, Dublin 12).
*Vulcan Model Engineering* — (36 Northampton Street, Birmingham 18).
*Weald Models*
*Westward Scale Models* — (Crow Meadow, Kingswood, Wotton-under-Edge, Glos). Cast and etched 4mm.
*Wills Finecast* — (Forest Row, Sussex). Cast 4mm

## Wheels

*Hamblings* — 29 Cecil Court, Charing Cross Road, London WC2
*Alan Gibson* — The Bungalow, Church Road, Lingwood, Norwich, Norfolk.
*Romford* — W&H Models, 14 New Cavendish Street, London W1.
*Ulstrascale*
*Mike Sharman* — 10 Swindon Road, Cricklade, Swindon, Wilts.

## Name and Number Plates

*CGW* — C. Gordon Watford, 21 High Street, Billingborough, Sleaford, Lincs.
*King's Cross* — Model Railway (Manufacturing) Co, 14 York Way, King's Cross, London N1.
*Jackson-Evans* — 4 Dartmouth Road, Coventry.
*LFC* — LFC Models, Grandsire Well, New Road, Holmfirth, Huddersfield.

## Transfers and Lining

*Kemco* — 82 Delce Road, Rochester, Kent.
*Kingsprint* — Model Railway (Manufacturing) Co, 14 York Way, King's Cross, London N1.
*Mabex* — 15 Coastguard Square, Barden Road, Eastbourne, Sussex.
*PC Models* — 2 Marsh Lane, Erdington, Birmingham.
*SMS* — PO Box 16, Glasgow.

## Paints

*Compucolour*
*Hobbycolour* — EAMES/King's Cross, as for Kingsprint transfers.
*Floquil/Poly-S* — Agent — Victors, 166 Pentonville Road, Islington, London N1.
*Humbrol* — Marfleet, Hull.
*Precision Paints* — PO Box 43, Cheltenham, Glos.
*Scalecoat* — See Floquil above.

## Airbrushes

*Badger* — Morris & Ingram, 156 Stanley Green Road, Poole, Dorset.
*DeVilbiss* — Ringwood Road, Bournemouth, Dorset.
*Efbe* — Frisk Products, 40a Parsons Head, West Croydon, Surrey.
*Humbrol* — Marfleet, Hull.
*Paasche* — Microflame (UK) Ltd, Abbots Hall, Vinces Road, Rickinghall, Diss, Norfolk.

## Propellants

See Badger, Frisk and Humbrol as above.

## General Retailers

*W & H Models* — 14 New Cavendish Street, London W1.
*Hamblings* — 29 Cecil Court, Charing Cross Road, London WC2.
*EAMES* — 24 Tudor Road, Reading, Berks.
*King's Cross* — 14 York Way, King's Cross, London N1.
*Hobbytime* — 5 and 7 Ravenswood Crescent, West Wickham, Kent.
*Holt Model Railways* — Bishopton Road, Bishopton, Gower, Swansea.
*West Coast Kit Centre* — 15 Oxford Street, Weston-super-Mare, Avon.
*M. G. Sharp Models* — 712 Attercliffe Road, Sheffield.

# NEW! — "The Merchant Navy" Class as rebuilt — from In 'OO' Gauge featuring the new 5-pole motor! . . .

**KEYSER MODEL KITS**

During 1956-59, all 30 locos of this class were rebuilt from Bulleid's original 1941 design. Following conversion, in fact, little remained of the first loco, except for the characteristic 'Box Pok' wheels. Destined to haul the crack expresses of the Southern Region, all saw service with British Rail until the end of the steam era.

## Two Superb kits from KEYSER MODEL KITS

**No. L49 — In standard silver series Kit — "Port Line"** — white metal casting, *complete* with 5-pole motor, chassis, wheels and body details — **£58.00** RRP.

**No. GK49 IN GOLD SERIES KIT — "Clan Line"** — white metal casting, *complete* with 5-pole motor, pre-assembled valve gear and chassis, pre-formed handrails with metal supports, pre-formed pipework, pre-drilled holes in castings, *sprung* brass buffers, including livery transfers, etched name-plate and express header board — 'Golden Arrow'. **£98.00** RRP

THE *FIRST* SUPER QUALITY *GOLD SERIES KIT* INCORPORATING SUPER-DETAILING FEATURES!

ARE AVAILABLE AT YOUR LOCAL MODEL SHOP

*Distributed by:*
**M&R (Model Railways) Ltd.,
27 Richmond Place, Brighton.**